Anger Management for Parents

How to Stop Losing Your Temper and Understand What Causes Explosive and Reactive Parenting

Rocky Hunter

© **Copyright 2023 - All rights reserved.**

The content contained within this book may not be reproduced, duplicated or transmitted without direct written permission from the author or the publisher.

Under no circumstances will any blame or legal responsibility be held against the publisher, or author, for any damages, reparation, or monetary loss due to the information contained within this book, either directly or indirectly.

Legal Notice:

This book is copyright protected. It is only for personal use. You cannot amend, distribute, sell, use, quote or paraphrase any part, or the content within this book, without the consent of the author or publisher.

Disclaimer Notice:

Please note the information contained within this document is for educational and entertainment purposes only. All effort has been executed to present accurate, up to date, reliable, complete information. No warranties of any kind are declared or implied. Readers acknowledge that the author is not engaged in the rendering of legal, financial, medical or professional advice. The content within this book has been derived from various sources. Please consult a licensed professional before attempting any techniques outlined in this book.

By reading this document, the reader agrees that under no circumstances is the author responsible for any losses, direct or indirect, that are incurred as a result of the use of the information contained within this document, including, but not limited to, errors, omissions, or inaccuracies.

Table of Contents

INTRODUCTION 1

CHAPTER 1: UNDERSTANDING ANGER 5

The Beast Known as Anger 6
The Different Faces of Anger 7
    Passive Aggression 8
    Open Aggression 8
    Assertive Anger 9
Do I Have an Anger Problem? 10
    Signs of Anger Problems 10
    Physical Symptoms of Anger 11
The Harm of Angry Parenting 12
Stories 14
Let the Work Begin: Is My Anger a Problem? 15
    Identifying Anger Triggers 15
    Assessing the Impact of Anger on Parenting 16
    Reflecting on Your Anger Management Skills 16
    Goal Setting 16

CHAPTER 2: PLEASE STOP YELLING—THE UNINTENTIONAL VICTIMS OF ANGER 19

Your Anger Affects Your Children More Than You Know 19
    How Your Anger Makes Them Feel Devalued 20
    How Your Anger Causes Their Behavior Issues to Worsen 21
    How Your Anger Affects Brain Development 21
    How Your Anger Affects Their Mental Health 22
Breaking the Cycle of Anger 22
    Teaching Your Child to Express Themself 23
    Modeling Behavior 23
    Anger and Genetics 24
Story 24
Let the Work Begin: Writing a Letter to Your Inner Child 27
Reclaim the Joy of Childhood 28

CHAPTER 3: TRIGGERS—THE WHY OF ANGER 31

THE HOW AND WHY OF TRIGGERS 31
- Childhood Trauma 31
- Feeling Unheard or Undervalued.. 32
- Noticing Things About Ourselves We Don't Like in Our Children... 33
- Natural Survival Instinct 34
- Difficulty Managing Your Emotions...................................... 34
- Higher Rates of Stress and Anxiety in Adults 35

COMBATING TRIGGERS... 36
- Stay in the Present Moment 36

COMMON PARENTING TRIGGERS AND HOW TO DEAL WITH THEM 39
- Whining 39
- Disrespect 40
- Tantrums 40
- Physical Aggression 40
- Sibling Fights 41
- Spills and Messes 41

STORY.. 42
LET THE WORK BEGIN: MY TRIGGERS 43

CHAPTER 4: TAME THE INNER CRITIC—IMPROVING YOUR SELF-TALK 47

IT STARTS WITH HOW YOU TALK TO YOURSELF..................................... 47
- The Destructive Nature of Negative Self-Talk........................ 48
- How It Triggers Feelings of Anger...................................... 48
- This Leads to Reacting Poorly to Others 49

TRANSITIONING TO POSITIVE SELF-TALK 50
- Improving Self-Talk 51

STORY.. 57
LET THE WORK BEGIN: CHALLENGING MY NEGATIVE THOUGHTS WORKSHEET ... 58

CHAPTER 5: LET'S TALK—EFFECTIVE COMMUNICATION MATTERS 61

THE IMPORTANCE OF PARENT-CHILD COMMUNICATION 61
THE "HOW TO'S" OF EFFECTIVE COMMUNICATION 63
TIPS FOR TALKING TO YOUR CHILD... 64
GETTING YOUR CHILDREN TO LISTEN... WITHOUT YOU YELLING 66
STORY.. 68
LET THE WORK BEGIN: THE NO YELLING CHALLENGE 69

CHAPTER 6: LEADING WITH LOVE—POSITIVE PARENTING 73

POSITIVE PARENTING EXPLAINED.. 74

 Qualities of Positive Parenting 74
 How Can I Implement Positive Parenting? 76
 DISCIPLINE IN POSITIVE PARENTING 77
  A Definition of Positive Discipline 78
  What It Teaches Our Children 79
 KEY FEATURES OF POSITIVE DISCIPLINE TO IMPLEMENT................................. 80
 STORY 83
 LET THE WORK BEGIN: CHARTS GALORE! 84

CHAPTER 7: YOU TOO NEED A BREAK—THE IMPORTANCE OF SELF-CARE 87

 YOU GOTTA GET RID OF THE GUILT 87
 SELF-CARE TIPS FOR MOMS AND DADS 89
 FORMS OF SELF-CARE 90
  Physical Self-Care 91
  Emotional Self-Care 93
  Social Self-Care 95
  Spiritual self-care 96
 STORY 98
 LET THE WORK BEGIN: A WEEK OF WRITING IT OUT 99

CHAPTER 8: IN THE HEAT OF THE MOMENT—STOPPING ANGER IN ITS TRACKS 101

 FIRST, DON'T BE SO HARD ON YOURSELF! 102
 SECONDLY, CUT YOURSELF SOME SLACK 103
 THIRD, GIVE YOURSELF A PARENT TIME-OUT 105
 FINALLY, DISTRACT YOURSELF 107
 STORY 109
 LET THE WORK BEGIN: DISTRACT YOURSELF WITH HOBBIES 110

CHAPTER 9: BREATHE IN, BREATHE OUT—THE POWER OF MINDFULNESS 113

 WHY MINDFULNESS IS MORE THAN A "NEW AGE" BUZZWORD 113
 MINDFUL PARENTING 115
 BREATHING YOUR WAY TO CALM 118
  Benefits of Breathing Exercises for Children and Teens 119
  Tips for Going Through Breathing Exercises with Children and Teens 119
  Breathing Exercises 120
 THE POWER OF MEDITATION 121
 STORY 123

LET THE WORK BEGIN: BELLY BREATHING TO TAME THE BEAST INSIDE 124
GUIDED MEDITATION FOR MOM AND DAD 125

CHAPTER 10: MOVING FORWARD—HEALING WITH YOUR CHILDREN 129

- IT BEGINS WITH "I'M SORRY" 129
- TRANSITION INTO DOS AND DON'TS OF APOLOGIZING TO CHILDREN 131
  - *Dos* 131
  - *Don'ts* 132
- MOVING FORWARD... TOGETHER 134
- STORY 135
- LET THE WORK BEGIN: SORRY 137
  - *Worksheet* 138

CONCLUSION 141

REFERENCES 143

A Free Gift to All My Readers!

As a thank you and an attempt to provide you with the most value possible, I would love to send you a free copy of my eBook Mind Blowing Facts For Smart Kids!

To receive your complimentary copy now, please visit *www.rocky-hunter.com*

Introduction

The way we talk to our children becomes their inner voice. —Peggy O'Mara

When I was young, I can recall my parents resorting to yelling as their primary form of discipline. Every time my siblings and I misbehaved, my parents would raise their voices and reprimand us for our actions. It was a constant cycle of "Don't do this…"; "Stay away from that…"; "Leave your brother alone…"

As I grew older, I started to realize that I was emulating this behavior. Whenever I encountered something I didn't like, I would immediately get angry and lash out. It wasn't until I was in my late teens and early 20s that I began to take notice of my actions and how they were impacting my life and relationships.

Then, one day, while studying different cultures in a class, I came across a book about Inuit culture. I learned that the Inuit people discipline their children without anger. Instead, they used playful and creative methods to teach their children how to control their emotions and behavior.

This book described the ways in which the Inuit people parented, and I was inspired to incorporate their ideas into my own parenting. Through my own journey of learning to manage my anger, I have come to understand that anger management is a crucial skill for any parent.

I'm a father of two, so I understand how challenging it can be to manage the stress and frustration that come with raising children. We love them more than anything, but sometimes it feels like they can push us to our limits.

I have seen firsthand the impact that anger can have on our relationships with our children, and I believe in actively seeking ways to become better parents. I lead parenting classes where I teach a wide array of conscious parenting techniques from the very beginning to dads and moms who think they're doing everything wrong.

My motivation behind writing this book is to reach parents who feel like they are perpetuating the cycle of anger that was passed down to them. I understand how difficult this can be and want to provide real-life ways to improve their reactions to and relationships with their children.

In this book, I will share techniques that I have learned through my years of parenting and teaching. These techniques include how to get to the root of your anger, ways to recognize and deal with triggers, how to practice positive parenting, and how to incorporate mindfulness into your parenting. By reading this book, you'll learn shortcuts to manage your anger and develop a stronger, healthier relationship with your children. As a fellow parent, this anger management guide is my gift to you.

Thanks for purchasing my book. After you finish reading the book, I would really appreciate it if you could help spread the word and leave a review on Amazon so we can reach a greater audience and help them in the same way that we have hopefully helped you. If you wish to leave a review, you can use your mobile phone's camera to scan the QR code provided below and then click on the book to access it. Once you click on the book, you will find a button to leave a review. If you do not own a smartphone, please search for my book on Amazon and take 60 seconds to leave a review. You are amazing!

Chapter 1:

Understanding Anger

Am I just an unhappy person... or is there something more to my anger?

Am I just not cut out for parenting?

Parenting can be incredibly rewarding, but it's no easy feat. It can be frustrating, overwhelming, and downright infuriating at times. The days when kids don't seem to listen are the ones during which frustrations pile up—the bad days that feel like everything is going wrong! During such moments, it is common to feel like your anger is taking control of you. You might find yourself asking, "Why can't my child just listen?" or "Why am I always so angry?"

The first step in getting a handle on your anger is to understand it. That's why this chapter takes a deep dive into anger, exploring what it is, what causes it, and what its different types and stages are. We'll also look at the physical and emotional symptoms of anger, helping you recognize when you're getting triggered and giving you strategies to calm yourself down before things escalate. By the end of this chapter, you'll have a much better understanding of your anger and how to begin managing it. Take a deep breath, and let's get to the root of this emotional beast.

The Beast Known as Anger

Anger is a strong emotion that can range from mild irritation to intense rage. It often arises when something goes wrong, or someone wrongs you, causing feelings of stress and frustration. Essentially, anger is the feeling of being upset with someone or something that you believe has been intentionally done wrong by you. It is an emotion that is characterized by antagonism toward someone, or something you feel has deliberately wronged you. Anger can manifest itself in many different ways, including physical and verbal aggression, passive aggression, and emotional withdrawal. It's important to note that anger is a normal and healthy emotion when expressed appropriately, but excessive anger can cause problems in both personal and professional relationships. In summary, anger can be described as a beast that lurks within, waiting to be unleashed when triggered by certain events or situations.

Anger is an emotion that is part of the body's "fight, flight, or freeze" system, a natural, instinctive response to threats. It has been refined throughout human history and is associated with basic survival instincts. When we experience anger, it can feel like an intense physical response, with our heart rate increasing, our muscles tensing, and our blood pressure rising. These responses are designed to prepare our bodies for action, to help us respond quickly and effectively to perceived threats.

Anger helped our ancestors respond to danger and protect themselves and their families. However, in modern times, anger can be triggered by a wide range of stimuli, and excessive anger can cause problems in our personal and professional lives.

While anger can be a normal and healthy emotion in some situations, it can also be destructive and harmful when it is not properly managed. Chronic anger can have negative consequences for both physical and mental health, including increased risk for heart disease, depression, and anxiety.

It's important to understand that anger is not inherently bad or wrong. It's a natural emotion that can be helpful in certain situations. However, when anger is not managed appropriately, it can lead to negative consequences for both the individual and those around them. Learning to recognize the signs of anger and developing effective coping strategies can help individuals manage their emotions and maintain healthy relationships.

To summarize, anger is a normal emotion that is integrated into the body's natural "fight or flight" response system. It's tied to basic survival and was honed over the course of human history. While it can be a normal and healthy emotion in some situations, excessive anger can cause problems in our personal and professional lives. Learning to recognize the signs of anger and developing effective coping strategies can help individuals manage their emotions and maintain healthy relationships.

The Different Faces of Anger

Anger is like an onion, with many layers and nuances that make it a complex and multi-faceted emotion. Sometimes, it comes on like a tornado, leaving destruction in its path. Other times, it simmers below the surface, waiting to boil over. In this section, we explore the different faces of anger, discussing the various forms it can take and the ways it can manifest in the way we raise our children. From the explosive anger that erupts suddenly and without warning to the passive-aggressive anger that lingers beneath the surface, understanding anger and how it presents itself equips us to change our parenting approaches and become calmer even in angering situations. Let's peel back the layers and discover the many faces of anger together!

Passive Aggression

Passive aggression is a form of anger where negative emotions are expressed indirectly instead of being confronted openly. It is often characterized by subtle, indirect behaviors that are meant to convey dissatisfaction, frustration, or anger without overtly expressing these emotions. Passive-aggressive behavior may occur as a result of various factors, such as fear of confrontation, a desire for control, or a belief that expressing anger is inappropriate or dangerous.

Procrastination, giving someone the quiet treatment, pouting, or purposefully forgetting something are a few instances of passive-aggressive behavior. It can have a significant impact on those around the individual, especially children. Passive-aggressive behavior can lead to a breakdown in communication and trust in relationships and can create an environment of tension, stress, and frustration.

Open Aggression

On the other hand, open aggression involves the direct expression of anger in a way that can be both verbal and physical. It can range from shouting, yelling, and threatening behavior to physical aggression, such as hitting or throwing objects. This type of anger is often fueled by a sense of frustration, fear, or perceived injustice.

Open aggression can be a manifestation of explosive anger, which refers to a sudden and intense outburst that may occur in response to a triggering event or situation. While open aggression and explosive anger can be related, they represent different aspects of the complex emotion of anger, so you shouldn't confuse them.

Explosive anger isn't always tied to aggression; it can also manifest as internal turmoil, such as intense feelings of anger, irritability, or rage, without any external display of aggression. This type of explosive anger can be just as harmful to your mental and physical health as open aggression and can lead to a range of negative outcomes, including a strained relationship with your children, decreased job performance, and even health problems such as high blood pressure or heart disease.

Children who witness aggressive behavior from their parents may become more likely to exhibit aggressive behavior themselves. They may also experience feelings of fear, anxiety, or trauma, which can have lasting effects on their mental health and well-being.

Assertive Anger

Expressing anger assertively is considered a healthy way to communicate this emotion. It involves communicating your feelings and needs in a calm, clear, and respectful manner. This form of anger helps you assert yourself and stand up for your rights without resorting to aggression or passive aggression.

Signs of assertive anger include clear communication, active listening, and the ability to negotiate and compromise. It is a common way of expressing anger, and research has shown that it can be an effective way of reducing stress, improving relationships, and promoting personal growth.

Understanding the different types of anger helps you to recognize your own anger patterns and develop healthy ways of expressing this emotion. By using assertive anger, you can model healthy communication and conflict resolution skills to your children, helping them to grow into emotionally healthy and resilient adults.

Do I Have an Anger Problem?

After breaking countless cups and dishes in her home, one woman came to me for help with her anger issues. She is a mother of two active toddlers who run around all day and sing nursery rhymes all night. If you get the picture, you may agree it's understandable to shatter a glass or two while yelling your head off for tiny humans to stop making noise or chasing each other during mealtimes.

However, normal situations that trigger anger don't become excessive. When this emotion seems to overcome you, and you go the extra mile regardless of the trigger or surroundings, that's a red flag; you may have an anger problem.

Signs of Anger Problems

Anger is a normal and natural emotion, but when it is expressed inappropriately, it can lead to various problems in our personal and professional lives. Here are some signs that may indicate an anger problem:

- Feeling angry frequently and intensely, even over small matters.

- Difficulty controlling or managing your anger, leading to aggressive behavior, such as yelling, throwing objects, or physical violence.

- Feeling easily irritated or frustrated, especially in situations where things do not go as planned.

- Experiencing frequent outbursts of anger, which can include verbal or physical aggression.

- Others may feel uncomfortable around you or avoid you altogether, as they feel like they need to walk on eggshells.

- Tendency to start arguments or escalate conflicts, even when the situation does not warrant it.

- Difficulty expressing emotions other than anger or feeling that you need to resort to anger to get your point across.

It is essential to understand that everyone experiences anger differently, and not all of these signs may apply to you. However, if you find that these signs are interfering with your daily life and relationships, it may be time to seek professional help.

Physical Symptoms of Anger

Apart from emotional and behavioral indicators, anger can also display physical symptoms.

Some common physical symptoms of anger include:

- chest tightness or pain
- clenched jaw or fists
- feeling hot or flushed
- increased heart rate
- muscle tension or soreness

These physical symptoms are a result of the body's fight-or-flight response, where the body prepares to either confront or flee from a perceived threat. These symptoms can be helpful in short bursts when dealing with a real threat, but if they persist, they can lead to chronic stress and health problems.

It is important to recognize these physical symptoms as a warning sign that you need to take steps to manage your anger before it becomes problematic. Several techniques and strategies can aid in the management of anger, including cognitive-behavioral therapy, relaxation methods, and attending anger management courses. With the right support and tools, it is possible to manage anger in a healthy and constructive way.

The Harm of Angry Parenting

Reactive parenting is parenting that is based on immediate reactions to a child's behavior and emotions, often caused by anger, frustration, or fear. This type of parenting is often triggered by stressors outside of parenting, such as work or financial difficulties. Reactive parenting can have several negative consequences for both parents and children.

One of the main harms of angry parenting is that it upsets both the parent and the child. When parents lash out in anger, it can create a sense of fear and insecurity in the child, and the child may start to avoid the parent or withdraw from them. Additionally, when a parent reacts angrily to a child's behavior, it can cause the parent to feel guilty and remorseful, further straining the parent-child relationship.

Angry parenting may also escalate bad situations and behaviors. For example, if a child is acting out, an angry parent may respond by yelling, which can escalate the situation and make the child's behavior worse. This can lead to a vicious cycle where the child's behavior continues to escalate, and the parent becomes increasingly angry and frustrated.

Raising children in angry atmospheres has lasting effects on their mental, emotional, and cognitive development. Children who are exposed to angry parenting may experience anxiety, depression, and behavioral problems. Additionally, angry parenting can impair a child's ability to regulate their emotions and develop healthy coping strategies.

Angry parenting also blurs judgment and causes overreactions. When parents are angry, they may be more likely to overreact to a situation and make decisions that they would not make if they were calm. This can lead to consequences that are disproportionate to the situation, such as harsh punishments or impulsive decisions.

Furthermore, angry parenting can stop parents from thinking before they speak. When parents are angry, they may say hurtful things to their children that they do not really mean. This can damage the parent-child relationship and create lasting emotional scars for the child.

In extreme cases, angry parenting even causes parents to do things that they would not typically do, such as physical or verbal abuse. It is essential to seek help if you find that you are struggling with angry parenting and cannot manage your emotions effectively. Seeking help can prevent long-term harm to both you and your child.

Stories

One mother I worked with came to me because she was feeling the physical effects of her anger more and more. She would often experience chest tightness and shortness of breath, which was understandably concerning for her. She also noticed that her anger was starting to affect her relationships, particularly with her children. Her child was starting to act out at school, and she felt helpless to stop it. She didn't understand where her anger was coming from or how to control it.

As we worked together, we uncovered that this mother had a lot of unprocessed emotions from her own childhood that were manifesting as anger. She also had a lot of stressors in her life that were contributing to her feelings of overwhelm and frustration. We worked on identifying her triggers and developing coping strategies to help her manage her anger at the moment. Furthermore, we worked together to devise long-term solutions to tackle the underlying causes of her anger.

Another father I worked with was struggling to control his anger with his teenage son. He would often blow up at his son over small things, which made his son feel like he couldn't do anything right. The father recognized that his behavior was damaging their relationship, but he didn't know how to stop it.

Through our work together, we discovered that the father had a lot of unaddressed anger toward his own father. He realized that he was projecting that anger onto his son and that his outbursts were more about his own unresolved emotions than anything his son was doing. Together, we worked on developing healthy ways for the father to process his emotions and communicate with his son in a more constructive way.

In both of these examples, the parents were able to make significant progress in managing their anger and improving their relationships with their children. It's important to remember that anger is a normal emotion, but when it becomes overwhelming or starts to negatively impact your life, it's time to seek help. With the right tools and support, it's possible to overcome even the most challenging anger issues.

Let the Work Begin: Is My Anger a Problem?

Anger can make us feel like fire-breathing dragons, and we have all been there as parents; whether it's because your little one won't stop jumping on the couch or because they have drawn on the walls with permanent markers. It's natural to get frustrated and feel angry from time to time, but how do we know when our anger is a problem? Well, if you find yourself smashing things or spitting fire like a dragon, it might be time to take a step back and ask yourself: Is my anger a problem? Let's take a closer look at how our anger affects parenting and how we can work toward better anger management skills.

Identifying Anger Triggers

1. What situations or behaviors tend to trigger your anger as a parent? List at least three.

2. How do you typically respond when you are triggered? (For example, do you yell, become silent, or physically lash out?)

Assessing the Impact of Anger on Parenting

1. How has your anger affected your relationship with your child(ren)?

2. In what ways has your anger impacted your child(ren)'s behavior or emotions?

3. How has your anger influenced your ability to effectively communicate with your child(ren)?

4. How has your anger impacted your ability to provide a safe and nurturing environment for your child(ren)?

Reflecting on Your Anger Management Skills

1. Do you feel that your current anger management skills are effective in helping you manage your anger as a parent? Why or why not?

2. What strategies have you tried in the past to manage your anger? Did they work? Why or why not?

3. Based on your answers to the previous questions, what skills or strategies do you need to develop or improve to better manage your anger as a parent?

Goal Setting

1. What is your goal for managing your anger as a parent?

2. What specific actions can you take to work toward this goal? List at least three.

In this chapter, we covered what anger is, how it feels, and the ways in which it affects our children and us. We discussed the various types of anger and the different stages it can go through. Using interactive exercises, we also explored anger triggers and assessed the impact of anger on our parenting.

We have learned that anger can have unintended consequences on our children and are about to move on to the next chapter. In chapter 2, we will delve deeper into how our anger can affect our children. Then we will cover some strategies for managing anger in a way that minimizes its impact on our little ones. Let's dive in and learn how to become better parents by managing our anger effectively.

Chapter 2:

Please Stop Yelling—The Unintentional Victims of Anger

Parenting is a beautiful task that has its highs and lows. It may be filled with all kinds of emotions, from precious joy to losing your cool. But what happens when you lose your cool and you can't control your emotions? You will obviously start yelling at your child, especially if they are doing something you told them not to do over and over again. You probably know that your anger is not beneficial to your children, but how does it affect them? Does getting mad at them really solve the problem at hand? Let's get started and discover how your anger impacts your kids.

Your Anger Affects Your Children More Than You Know

As parents, we all strive to provide a loving and nurturing environment for our children. However, there are times when our anger unintentionally seeps into our interactions with them, causing more harm than we realize. Children are highly impressionable and tend to absorb everything in their surroundings, including how we convey our emotions. This is why it's essential to understand how anger can impact our children and their well-being.

In this section, we will explore the ways in which your anger can affect your children, including the short-term and long-term consequences. You will also discover practical strategies to help you recognize when your anger is negatively impacting your child. Remember, you have a tremendous impact on your child's emotional development, and your parenting journey involves ensuring that your anger doesn't get in the way of your young one's happiness and success.

How Your Anger Makes Them Feel Devalued

Parents who express their anger toward their children may not realize the impact it may have on their child's self-worth and self-esteem. Yelling at your children is not an effective way to discipline them because it can make them feel devalued and unimportant. If you frequently expose your children to parental anger, they may feel like they are not respected or valued, leading to a sense of anxiety and fear. As a result, this can have a considerable impact on their emotional and mental well-being; and may lead to difficulties in other areas of their life, such as school, friendships, and other relationships. They may start to feel like they are not worthy of their parent's love and attention, leading to low self-esteem and a lack of confidence. Think of it this way: If you are constantly being yelled at by your boss at work, it may make you feel less important. This can lead to negative thoughts and feelings about yourself, making it harder for you to thrive and succeed at your workplace.

How Your Anger Causes Their Behavior Issues to Worsen

Yelling and expressing anger toward children may not only make them feel devalued, but it may also worsen their behavioral issues. Studies observed that frequent anger outbursts from parents can make it harder for children to regulate their emotions, leading to more behavioral problems such as acting out or being disobedient (Wang & Kenny, 2013). This means that if your child grows up in the shadows of parental anger, they may mimic that behavior and become angry or aggressive themselves. Over time, this may make it harder for your child to trust and communicate with you, leading to a cycle of negative behavior. If your child does not learn how to regulate their emotions, it can also lead to problems with mental health, school, and other areas of their life. When you address your own anger management issues and teach your child healthy coping skills, you may help prevent negative behavior and promote positive interactions.

How Your Anger Affects Brain Development

Exposing your children to your anger may also have a significant impact on their brain development. Research shows that chronic exposure to stress may affect the development of the prefrontal cortex, the part of the brain responsible for impulse control and decision-making (McKlveen et al., 2016). This can lead to difficulty with learning, memory, and attention, as well as difficulty with social and emotional functioning. Over time, chronic exposure to stress can lead to long-term changes in the brain, making it harder for your child to succeed in school, work, and other areas of their life. By reducing stress in your household and promoting healthy coping mechanisms, you may help prevent long-term damage to your child's brain development.

How Your Anger Affects Their Mental Health

Parental anger may also have a significant impact on your child's mental health. Studies have shown that yelling at children may have negative effects on their development and well-being. Yelling can lead to increased anxiety, depression, aggression, and other mental health issues (Norman et al., 2012). Your child may also struggle with self-esteem and self-worth. Furthermore, your child may feel like they are responsible for your anger, and they may experience feelings of guilt and shame, further exacerbating their mental health issues. In addition, regularly yelling at your children may desensitize them to it over time, leading to a higher tolerance for conflict and aggression in their future relationships. It's important for parents and caregivers to find alternative ways to discipline and communicate with their children that do not involve yelling or other forms of verbal abuse. It's important for you to recognize the impact of your anger on your children's mental health and to seek help and support if needed.

Breaking the Cycle of Anger

Now that you know how your anger may affect your children if projected. You may be wondering where the anger comes from? Does it run in the family? Is it possible to break the cycle? Below, you'll learn more.

Anger sometimes runs in families. It is not uncommon for different people in the same family to express anger in similar ways. If you grew up with angry parents, you are more likely to become an angry parent too. This cycle of anger can be difficult to break, but it is not impossible. If you recognize that you have an anger problem, you can take steps to address it, such as seeking therapy or anger management classes. By doing so, you may not only help yourself but also prevent your children from inheriting your anger issues.

Teaching Your Child to Express Themself

One way to break the cycle of anger is to teach your child how to express themselves in a healthy way. Children who are taught how to communicate their feelings are less likely to become angry and more likely to have positive relationships. As a parent, you can model healthy communication by listening to your child, asking open-ended questions, and using "I" statements when expressing your own feelings. It is also important to encourage your child to express themselves through activities such as drawing or writing, which can be a healthy outlet for their emotions.

Modeling Behavior

Modeling, or learning by example, is a powerful teaching tool that plays a key role in children's learning and development. Children often learn more from what they see and experience in their environment than what they are explicitly taught. Modeling may help children acquire new skills and knowledge and develop positive behaviors and attitudes (Bandura, 2008).

If you are an angry and aggressive parent, then your children are more likely to exhibit the same behavior. On the other hand, if you model healthy communication and positive coping mechanisms, your children are more likely to adopt those behaviors. As a parent, it is important to be mindful of your behavior and how it may be affecting your child. By modeling healthy coping mechanisms and positive behavior, you can break the cycle of anger and prevent your child from inheriting your anger issues.

Anger and Genetics

There is evidence to suggest that anger may have a genetic component to it, and this is especially true for men (National Institute of Health, 2015). However, genetics is not the only factor that contributes to anger expression. Environmental factors, such as exposure to stress and trauma, can also play a significant role. While anger may have a genetic component, it is important for you to recognize your own role in promoting healthy emotional regulation in your children. By modeling healthy coping mechanisms and providing a safe and supportive environment, you may help your children develop healthy emotional regulation skills.

It is up to you to break the cycle, and the first step in doing so is healing your inner child.

If you grew up in an environment where anger was prevalent, it might be necessary to heal your inner child before you effectively break the cycle of anger. This may involve seeking therapy, practicing self-care, and confronting past trauma. By healing your inner child, you can learn to respond to situations in a healthy and productive way, which may have a positive impact on your child's emotional development. It is important to remember that breaking the cycle of anger is not a one-time event but rather a lifelong process of growth and self-improvement.

Story

As a parenting educator, I have seen all kinds of parents come through my classes. But there was something about this particular parent, let's call him Nikola. He was a big guy of Serbian descent with a shaved head and a stern expression. His broad shoulders and tense jaw suggested a man used to getting his way. His wife, let's call her Lara, was smaller, more delicate-looking, and wore a nervous expression that seemed to indicate she was intimidated by her husband.

When I approached Nikola after the class and asked him how he felt about the discussion on anger management, he looked at me in a certain way and replied, "What discussion?" he asked, his voice gruff. "I don't have a problem with anger. That's just how I was raised. It's what worked for me, and it's what works for my kids. I am only here because my wife insisted."

I could see his wife's face drop at the words, and I knew that Lara was worried about their children. She had talked to me before the class about how her husband's outbursts were affecting their family, but it was clear that Nikola brushed off her concerns.

Over the next few classes, I worked with the parents on techniques for managing stress, understanding the triggers for anger, and creating a calm home environment. At first, Nikola was skeptical, resistant, and even dismissive of some of the ideas. He didn't seem to take the class seriously and was more interested in playing with his phone than engaging in the discussion. But as the classes progressed, I could see a subtle shift in his attitude. He began to pay closer attention. He could ask and contribute to group discussions and participate in team-building activities.

One day, during a group exercise where we talked about our own childhood experiences with anger, Nikola surprised us all by opening up about his own upbringing. He shared how his father used to yell and spank him and how he had always thought that was normal as it was a way of discipline among most Serbians. He had never really questioned it until now. His wife was visibly moved by the confession, and she shared how she had been worried about their children and how they were being affected by Nikola's anger.

After the class, Nikola stayed behind and asked me more questions. He seemed genuinely interested in learning more about anger management techniques, and I could see the beginnings of a change in him. He was beginning to understand that the way he had been raised wasn't necessarily the best way to raise his own children. He had never really thought about it before, but he was starting to see how his behavior was affecting his family.

Over the next few weeks, Nikola became more engaged in the class and more willing to try new things. He started to practice relaxation techniques and breathing exercises, and he even tried talking to his children about how he was feeling instead of just yelling at them. It wasn't easy, and there were setbacks, but he was making progress.

At the end of the classes, Lara came up to me and thanked me for helping her family. She said she had noticed a big change in Nikola and how he interacted with their children. He was more patient, more understanding, and less quick to anger. She even said that their children had noticed a difference and seemed happier and more relaxed.

As for Nikola, he thanked me too. "I didn't think I had a problem with anger," he said, "but I guess I did. I'm glad my wife pushed me to attend these classes. I learned a lot, and I'm going to keep working on it." I could see a genuine smile on his face, and I knew that he was on the path to breaking the cycle of anger that had been a part of his life for so long.

Let the Work Begin: Writing a Letter to Your Inner Child

Now that you have learned about the impact of anger on your child's emotional and mental well-being; it's time to take action. One exercise that can help you on the path to healing is writing a letter to your inner child. The concept of your inner child refers to the part of your psyche that still carries the emotional scars and unresolved issues from your childhood. It's the part of you that experienced the anger and the pain that you may now be perpetuating with your own children. By acknowledging and healing your inner child, you can break the cycle of anger and create a healthier, happier family environment.

To begin this exercise, find a quiet and comfortable place where you can reflect on your thoughts and feelings. You can choose to write your letter by hand, or you can type it out on a computer. Here are some guidelines to help you get started:

1. Address your inner child by name. This can be any name that resonates with you. You may choose to use your childhood nickname, or you can create a new name that represents your inner child.

2. Begin by acknowledging the pain and hurt that your inner child experienced. This can be difficult, but it's important to be honest with yourself. Write about any experiences or situations that caused you to feel angry, scared, or alone as a child.

3. Offer words of comfort and support to your inner child. Imagine that you are talking to a younger version

of yourself. What would you say to comfort and reassure them? What kind words and actions would have made a difference to you as a child?

4. Write about the positive qualities that you have gained as a result of your childhood experiences. While it's important to acknowledge the pain, it's also important to recognize the strengths and resilience that you have developed as a result of your experiences. End your letter with a message of love and hope. This can be a simple sentence, such as "I love you, and I am committed to healing our pain and creating a better future for us."

Remember, this exercise is meant to be a tool for healing and self-reflection. Take your time with it, and don't worry about "getting everything right." The most important thing is to approach the exercise with an open heart and a willingness to connect with your inner child. By doing this exercise, you can gain a deeper understanding of the impact of your childhood experiences on your current parenting style. You can also begin to break the cycle of anger and create a more positive and loving relationship with your children. I wish you all the best on your path toward healing and personal development!

Reclaim the Joy of Childhood

After writing a letter to your childhood self and acknowledging the pain and hurt that you may have experienced, it's important to remember that childhood also has many joyful moments. As adults, we often become so consumed with work, responsibilities, and stress that we forget the simple pleasures of childhood. But by reconnecting with those moments of happiness, we can help heal our inner child and bring more joy into our lives.

Take some time to remember the fun parts of your childhood. Did you have any preferred toys or games as a child? Did you enjoy spending time outdoors or socializing with your friends? Maybe there was a special place that made you feel happy and safe, like a park or your grandparent's house.

Now, think about how you can bring those joyful moments back into your life. One possible approach could be to spend quality time with your children, engaging in playful activities with them. This can be a wonderful opportunity to reconnect with your own inner child and experience the joy of playfulness and curiosity. You might even rediscover some of your own childhood favorites, like playing tag or building a fort.

You may also do this exercise alone if your kids are unavailable. There are still plenty of ways to reconnect with the joy of childhood. You could try coloring in a coloring book, playing a board game, or simply going for a walk and taking in the sights and sounds around you. Whatever it is, make sure it's something that brings you joy and makes you feel carefree, even if it's just for a few minutes.

Reclaiming the joy of childhood can feel strange or uncomfortable at first, especially if you've been disconnected from that part of yourself for a long time. But it's important to remember that playfulness, curiosity, and joy are natural and healthy parts of being human. By rediscovering those elements of childhood, you can help heal your inner child and bring more happiness and fulfillment into your life.

So go ahead, take a break from the stress and responsibilities of adulthood, and let yourself be a kid again, even if it's just for a little while.

In this chapter, we explored how parental anger can affect children and how to break the cycle of anger that may have been passed down from previous generations. We discussed the importance of acknowledging your own inner child and how it may be impacting your parenting. It's crucial to understand that your own unresolved emotional wounds and past experiences can shape your reactions and behaviors toward your children. We offered exercises to help you connect with and heal your inner child, as well as to reclaim the joy of childhood.

In the next chapter, we will dive deeper into the roots of anger and what triggers it. Understanding the why and how of anger can help us take control of our emotional responses and develop healthier coping mechanisms. Buckle up.

Chapter 3:

Triggers—The Why of Anger

As a parent, have you ever found yourself reacting in anger toward your children, even when you know it's not the most helpful or effective way to deal with the situation? If so, you're not alone. In this chapter, we will explore the how and why of triggers of anger, including why we resort to anger almost every time and how to better manage our emotions.

The How and Why of Triggers

There are different factors that can trigger anger, including childhood trauma, feeling unheard or undervalued, and noticing things we don't like about ourselves in our children. These triggers may stem from our natural survival instinct. We will explore why it's important to understand them in order to better manage our emotions.

Childhood Trauma

Parenting anger triggers may often stem from childhood trauma, which can have lasting effects on an individual's mental health and behavior. Research shows that if you experienced maltreatment and trauma as a child, then you may be more likely to struggle with regulating your emotions as an adult (Perry, 2009; Dye, 2018). This may manifest in parenting as a tendency to resort to anger when faced with challenging behaviors from your children.

Childhood trauma can have a profound impact on our lives, including our ability to parent effectively. Traumatic experiences, such as abuse, neglect, or family conflict, may leave you feeling powerless, anxious, and fearful, which may make it difficult to manage your emotions and respond to your children's behavior in a calm and effective manner.

Feeling Unheard or Undervalued

As a parent, you want to feel that your opinions and concerns are heard and valued by those around you, including your partners, children, and other family members. However, when you've experienced childhood trauma, you may struggle to assert yourself in these relationships, leading to feelings of frustration, anger, and resentment. Children who experience trauma may feel like their needs and emotions are ignored or dismissed, leading to a deep sense of frustration and anger that can carry over into adulthood. Schore (2001) notes that a secure attachment relationship with a caregiver can help mitigate the effects of trauma and promote healthy emotional regulation, but when that attachment is disrupted by trauma, it can have long-term consequences.

Childhood trauma may impact your ability to feel heard or valued as a parent in the following ways:

- **Low self-esteem**: Childhood trauma may leave you with a deep sense of shame and self-doubt, making it difficult to assert your needs and boundaries as a parent.

- **Lack of support**: If you grew up in an environment where you didn't receive the support you needed, you might struggle to seek out support as a parent, leading to feelings of isolation and frustration.

- **Difficulty communicating**: Childhood trauma may also impact your ability to communicate effectively, making it hard to express your thoughts and feelings to your children.

When you feel unheard or undervalued, it can be easy to resort to anger as a way of expressing yourself. However, by recognizing these underlying issues and working to address them, you may learn to communicate more effectively and build stronger, more positive relationships with your children.

Noticing Things About Ourselves We Don't Like in Our Children

Another way that childhood trauma may contribute to parenting anger is by causing you to notice things about yourself you don't like in your children. For example, if you struggled with academic performance as a child, you may become angry and irritable when your child struggles in school as well. Here are some additional ways in which childhood trauma may affect your approach to parenting:

- **Unresolved emotions**: If you haven't processed your own emotions related to childhood trauma, you may struggle to respond to your children's behavior in a calm and compassionate manner.

- **Perfectionism**: If you grew up in an environment where you were expected to be perfect, you may be triggered by your child's mistakes or imperfections, leading to feelings of anger and disappointment.

- **Insecurity**: Childhood trauma can leave you feeling insecure about your parenting abilities, making it difficult to respond to your children's behavior in a confident and compassionate way.

By recognizing these triggers and working to address the underlying issues, we can learn to respond to our children's behavior in a more effective and compassionate way.

Natural Survival Instinct

Anger is a natural response to a perceived threat, which can be traced back to our survival instinct. The fight-or-flight response is a defense mechanism that has been ingrained in us as a way to protect ourselves from danger. When we perceive a threat, our brain releases adrenaline and other hormones that prepare our body to respond quickly. Anger is one of the responses that can help us fight off or flee from the threat. However, in modern society, this natural response can be triggered by situations that are not actually threatening or dangerous, leading to inappropriate or excessive anger.

Difficulty Managing Your Emotions

When you become angry, it can be difficult to manage your emotions effectively. This is because anger is a powerful emotion that can quickly take over and cloud your judgment. In addition, when you are angry, you are more likely to engage in negative self-talk, which can exacerbate your feelings of anger and make it even harder to control your emotions.

In addition, triggers for anger may lead to various physical and emotional symptoms that can be challenging to cope with. These symptoms may include increased heart rate, rapid breathing, and tense muscles. When you experience these symptoms, it can be hard to think clearly and respond in a calm and rational manner. Thus, learning to recognize and manage your anger triggers is essential for effective anger management.

Anger has a significant impact on your behavior and can lead to a poor adjustment in adulthood. For example, if you struggle with anger management, you may be more likely to engage in spousal abuse or aggression toward others. This may have a profound impact on your relationships and may lead to legal consequences.

Moreover, anger triggers can also affect your career achievement. Anger may lead to conflicts with coworkers or superiors, which may undermine your ability to succeed in your workplace. Additionally, anger may cause you to make impulsive decisions that may negatively impact your career goals.

Higher Rates of Stress and Anxiety in Adults

Anger may also have a significant impact on your mental health. Individuals who struggle with anger management may experience higher rates of stress and anxiety. This is because anger triggers can cause a range of physical symptoms, such as increased heart rate and tense muscles, which can be stressful and anxiety-provoking. Additionally, individuals who struggle with anger management may experience more conflict in their relationships, which can be a significant source of stress.

Anger may teach you to deal with your emotions in unhealthy ways. When you become angry, you may resort to outbursts or aggressive behavior as a way to express your feelings. This can pose a significant challenge, particularly in scenarios where it's necessary to handle conflicts in a composed and logical manner.

Moreover, when you use anger as a way to express your emotions, it can reinforce the belief that anger is an effective way to get what you want. This can create a cycle of anger triggers and outbursts that can be difficult to break. Thus, learning to manage our anger triggers effectively is essential for developing healthy emotional regulation skills and resolving conflicts in a constructive way.

Combating Triggers

The first step to combating triggers is to recognize when you are being triggered. Triggers can be different for everyone and can arise from past traumas or experiences like earlier discussed. You might feel powerless or overwhelmed in certain situations, and your emotions may spiral out of control. By acknowledging your triggers, you can identify patterns and learn to manage your emotions better.

Stay in the Present Moment

When you're triggered, you may find yourself ruminating about the past or worrying about the future. However, it's essential to stay in the present moment and focus on what is happening right now. Mindfulness techniques like deep breathing or meditation can help bring you back to the present moment and reduce anxiety and stress.

- **Take steps to combat an angry reaction**: If you feel like you're about to have an angry reaction, there are several things you can do to manage your emotions in a healthy way. This may include:

- **Ask why you're getting triggered**: Try to identify the reason why you're feeling triggered. Is it because of something that happened in your past, or is it related to your child's behavior? Once you know the reason, you can take steps to address it and manage your emotions better.

- **Start working on it**: Once you know what triggers you, it's time to start working on it. Seek support from a therapist or counselor who can help you understand your triggers and work through them. Talk to other parents or join a support group to gain insight into how others deal with similar challenges.

- **Know change is for the better**: Recognize that change is possible and necessary for your well-being and the well-being of your children. Making changes to how you manage your emotions may take time, but it will be worth it.

- **Start small**: To improve emotional regulation, start by implementing minor adjustments in your daily routine. For instance, set aside a few minutes every day for deep breathing exercises or meditation.. Make a conscious effort to stay calm and composed during stressful situations.

- **Work on healing**: Healing from past traumas or experiences is essential to manage triggers effectively. Consider seeking professional help to work through unresolved emotions and experiences that may be contributing to your triggers.

- **Take your time**: Managing triggers takes time and patience. Don't be hard on yourself if it takes longer than expected. Remember that healing is a process, and it's essential to be kind to yourself along the way.

- **Accept that you will make mistakes and apologize to your child when needed**. As human beings, making mistakes is an inherent part of our nature. When you make mistakes, it's important to apologize to your child and make things right. This shows your child that it's okay to make mistakes and that taking responsibility for our actions is crucial.

- **Understand childhood development**: Understanding your child's development can help you manage your expectations and respond to their behavior in a more constructive way. Knowing what typical behavior for their age is can help you avoid getting triggered and react in a more age-appropriate way.

- **Find a way to interrupt your reaction**: Identify ways to interrupt your angry reactions when you feel triggered. This could be taking a few deep breaths, counting to ten, or removing yourself from the situation until you can manage your emotions better.

- **Practice thought-stopping**: When you notice negative thoughts creeping in, practice thought-stopping. This involves stopping the negative thought and replacing it with a more positive one.

Common Parenting Triggers and How to Deal With Them

Triggers are part of parenthood; we all have experienced situations where our children's behavior can trigger an emotional reaction. Understanding the root cause of these behaviors and having strategies to manage them can be helpful in dealing with these common parenting triggers. In this section, we will explore some common parenting triggers and provide tips on how to deal with them.

Whining

Whining is a common behavior among young children, and it often triggers frustration and irritation in most parents. When your children whine, it is their way of expressing their needs and emotions. They might be tired, hungry, or frustrated and may not have the vocabulary to articulate their feelings. You may often react to whining with negative emotions, which can escalate the situation and lead to a power struggle.

Instead of reacting negatively, you may try to understand the reason behind the whining and respond accordingly. You should acknowledge your child's feelings and provide a calm and reassuring tone. For instance, instead of saying, "Stop whining," you may say, "I understand you are upset, and I am here to help you." You may also set clear boundaries and expectations about whining and teach your children more appropriate ways to express their emotions.

Disrespect

Disrespectful behavior is another common parenting trigger that you may encounter, and it can cause frustration and disappointment. Disrespectful behavior can include backtalk, rudeness, and defiance, among others. Children may exhibit this behavior due to their developmental stage, frustration, or lack of social skills.

Instead of taking this behavior personally, You may respond calmly and acknowledge your child's feelings. You may also establish clear boundaries and consequences for disrespectful behavior. You can teach your child alternative ways to express their emotions and communicate their needs.

Tantrums

Tantrums are common among young children and can be triggered by frustration, fatigue, hunger, or a need for control. Tantrums often manifest as crying, screaming, and kicking and can be challenging to handle. Your response to tantrums could potentially exacerbate the situation.

To effectively handle tantrums, it's crucial to remain composed and acknowledge your child's emotions. You may also try to distract your child's attention or provide alternative ways to manage their emotions, such as taking a break or deep breathing.

Physical Aggression

You can also face physical violence, which can be challenging to control.. Children may exhibit physical aggression due to their developmental stage, frustration, or lack of social skills.

Physical aggression can manifest as hitting, biting, or pushing, among others.

To deal with physical aggression, You should set clear boundaries and consequences for inappropriate behavior. You may also teach your child appropriate ways to express their emotions and communicate their needs by modeling nonviolent conflict resolution and avoiding using physical punishment.

Sibling Fights

Sibling rivalry is a common trigger for parents and can lead to frustration and stress. Siblings may fight due to jealousy, competition, or a need for attention. Your reactions to sibling fights can exacerbate the situation and lead to favoritism.

When dealing with sibling conflicts, it's important to remain impartial and refrain from favoring one child over the other. Again, establish clear boundaries and consequences for inappropriate behavior. It's beneficial to educate your children on conflict resolution strategies.

Spills and Messes

Spills and messes are common occurrences in a household with young children and can be a significant trigger. Your reaction to spills and messes can impact your child's behavior and self-esteem.

To deal with spills and messes, you should respond calmly and avoid overreacting. It's also valuable to teach your child the significance of cleanliness and maintaining a tidy environment.

Story

I had a client in one of my parenting classes who was a single mother struggling to control her anger toward her children. She was working hard to provide for them, but when her children fought, she would easily blow up, adding to her frustrations. She knew that her main trigger was her children fighting, while all she wanted was some rest after taking double shifts, but no matter how many times she calmly asked them to stop, the fighting would continue, and she would eventually lose her temper.

During our sessions, I presented various ways to work through her trigger, which she later implemented. These strategies include

Staying Calm: She learned that the calmer she was, the better she could manage her emotions. When her children started to fight, she took a deep breath and reminded herself to stay calm.

Acknowledging Feelings: She also learned to acknowledge her children's feelings. By listening to their concerns and showing empathy, she was able to diffuse their anger and help them understand each other better.

Setting Boundaries: She realized that it was important to set clear boundaries for her children. She explained that fighting was not acceptable and laid out the consequences for breaking this rule.

Encourage Problem-solving: Instead of intervening immediately, she encouraged her children to solve the problem themselves. She gave them time to come up with their own solutions, which helped them feel more empowered and responsible for their actions.

Provide Positive Reinforcement: When her children managed to resolve their issues without fighting, she praised their efforts and rewarded them with positive reinforcement. This encouraged them to continue using problem-solving skills in the future.

By incorporating these strategies consistently, she was able to manage her anger and respond more effectively to her children's fights. She found that her relationship with her children improved as they became more cooperative and understanding of each other. We also discussed how important it was for her to take care of herself, especially when she was feeling overwhelmed and tired.

She also realized that it was okay to ask for help and started reaching out to family and friends for support. With time and practice, she was able to overcome her trigger and create a more peaceful and loving environment for herself and her children.

Let the Work Begin: My Triggers

Think about situations that tend to make you feel frustrated, angry, or overwhelmed as a parent. Try to answer these questions below on a separate piece of paper below to help you identify your personal triggers.

1. What specific situations tend to trigger your anger as a parent?

2. How do you typically react when you feel triggered? Do you shout, criticize, or withdraw?

3. What are some physical and emotional signs that you are starting to feel triggered? For example, do you clench your fists, experience a racing heart, or start to feel hot?

4. What are some thoughts or beliefs that you have when you feel triggered? For example, do you tell yourself that your child is being disrespectful or that you're a bad parent?

5. What are some alternative ways you can respond when you feel triggered? You may attempt to calm yourself down by taking deep breaths, counting to ten, or simply detaching yourself from the situation.

6. What self-care practices can you engage in to help manage your triggers? For example, can you prioritize sleep, exercise, or time alone?

It's crucial to remember that understanding your triggers is the first step to successfully controlling them. With practice, you can learn to respond to your triggers in a more calm and effective way.

Parenting triggers are common and can cause you to react in ways you may regret. Some common parenting anger triggers may be from childhood trauma or your children's misconduct. While anger is a natural biological reaction, understanding why children behave in certain ways and how you tend to react can help you change their reactions.

Identifying personal anger triggers enables you to work through them and improve your parenting skills. Strategies for dealing with parenting triggers include staying calm, setting boundaries, validating feelings, and using positive reinforcement.

Mindfulness and self-care practices may also help you manage your emotions and respond more effectively to parenting triggers.

In the next chapter, we will explore how you can tame your inner critic and improve your self-talk.

Chapter 4:

Tame the Inner Critic—

Improving Your Self-Talk

As parents, we sometimes hold ourselves to impossibly high standards, and that's normal. We strive to be the perfect role models for our children, providing unconditional love, guidance, and support. But sometimes, our own self-doubt and negative self-talk can get in the way of being the awesome parent we want to be. That nagging voice inside our heads can turn every small mistake or imperfection into a monumental failure, eroding our self-esteem and confidence.

The good news is that with a bit of practice, you can learn to recognize and tame your inner critic. In this chapter, we will explore the destructive power of negative self-talk and how it can impact your parenting style. You will also discover practical strategies to turn those negative thoughts into positive ones. Learning to improve our self-talk helps boost your self-esteem and strengthen your relationship with your child.

It Starts With How You Talk to Yourself

As parents, we often hold ourselves to impossibly high standards, constantly striving to be the best we can be for our children. What do we get to do when we don't meet those expectations? We may find ourselves berating ourselves with negative self-talk, questioning our abilities and worth as a parent. And while we may think these critical thoughts are hidden away inside our heads, our children may be more perceptive than we realize.

Do our kids pick up on our self-doubt and self-criticism? And how does this inner dialogue impact our ability to parent effectively? In this chapter, we'll explore the concept of the inner critic, how it can manifest in our thoughts and behavior, and strategies for taming that inner voice and improving our self-talk.

The Destructive Nature of Negative Self-Talk

Negative self-talk can take many forms, such as self-blame, self-doubt, and self-criticism. Being in this state can result in feelings of worthlessness, hopelessness, and helplessness. The more you engage in negative self-talk, the more you reinforce unproductive beliefs about yourself and your abilities. Research shows that repetitive unconstructive thoughts, which are a hallmark of negative self-talk, may lead to increased stress, anxiety, and depression (Watkins, 2008).

How It Triggers Feelings of Anger

Negative self-talk may also trigger feelings of anger. If you indulge in negative self-talk, you might primarily concentrate on your perceived inadequacies and flaws. This, in turn, can give rise to emotions such as frustration, resentment, and anger. When you feel angry, you are more likely to react poorly to others, including your children. This can result in yelling, screaming, and even physical aggression.

This Leads to Reacting Poorly to Others

When you react poorly to your children, you not only hurt them but also damage your relationship with them. This doesn't only apply to your children but even to other external relationships that you have. You may feel guilty and ashamed of your behavior, which can further fuel your negative self-talk. This can create a cycle of negative behavior, negative thoughts, and negative feelings.

Unfortunately, it can be hard to get rid of this negative self-talk as you have grown to know it as a part of who you are—it is comforting.

It may be challenging to eradicate negative self-talk because it may be embedded deeply within you. You may become so accustomed to your negative thought patterns that they start to identify with you. It's like having a constant inner critic that judges and criticizes every action, thought, and decision. Negative self-talk can also be comforting because it provides a sense of familiarity and security, even though it's a toxic pattern.

But in reality, the inner critic steals from the present by keeping you stuck in the past!

Negative self-talk can also keep you stuck in the past by preventing them from fully engaging in the present. Constant self-criticism and self-doubt can make you second-guess your decisions and actions, leading to missed opportunities and regrets.

Transitioning to Positive Self-Talk

Acknowledging that negative self-talk is counterproductive and doesn't aid in accomplishing your objectives is crucial. To break this cycle, you need to transition into positive self-talk. Positive self-talk involves focusing on your strengths, successes, and positive qualities. Benefits of positive self-talk include:

- **Lower rates of depression**: Positive self-talk can help to reduce symptoms of depression and improve overall mood. When you focus on positive thoughts, it can be easier to see the good in a situation and feel more optimistic about the future.

- **Lower levels of distress**: When you engage in positive self-talk, you may experience less distress and anxiety in challenging situations. By focusing on the positive, you can feel more in control and better able to handle difficult circumstances.

- **Greater resistance to illness**: Research suggests that positive thinking can have a positive impact on physical health. People who engage in positive self-talk may have stronger immune systems and be more resistant to illness (Park et al., 2014).

- **Better psychological and physical well-being**: Self-talk that is constructive can enhance your well-being in general. When you focus on positive thoughts and beliefs, it can improve your mental and physical health, increase your happiness, and help you to feel more fulfilled.

- **Developing improved coping mechanisms during challenging times and stressful situations**: By focusing on positive self-talk, you can develop better coping skills for dealing with stress and difficult situations. When you believe in yourself and your abilities, you are better able to navigate challenges and bounce back from setbacks.

It's important to keep in mind that transitioning from negative self-talk to positive self-talk is a gradual process that may require time and practice. It's essential to be patient with yourself and concentrate on making progress rather than striving for perfection.

Improving Self-Talk

Negative thinking can take on many forms and can be detrimental to your mental health and well-being, as discussed in the previous section. This is especially true if you are already feeling overwhelmed and stressed out. By becoming aware of the different types of negative thinking, you can work toward reducing negative self-talk's impact on your life and improving your overall mental state.

Step One: Familiarize yourself with various forms of negative thinking

- **Blaming**: As a parent, it is often common to fall into the trap of blaming yourself for the challenges your children face. This kind of pessimistic thinking might make you feel guilty, ashamed, and frustrated.

- **Catastrophizing**: When things don't go as planned, it's easy to catastrophize and think that everything is going wrong. This type of negative thinking can cause you to feel helpless and anxious.

- **Filtering**: When one thinks negatively, they tend to ignore the positive parts of a situation and concentrate entirely on the bad ones. As a parent, this might involve overlooking the good things your children do and instead only focusing on the mistakes they make. Making an effort to reframe negative thoughts and centering your focus on positive aspects can be beneficial.

- **Magnifying**: Magnifying involves blowing things out of proportion and making a small problem seem much bigger than it actually is. When parenting, it's easy to get caught up in worrying about the little things, but it's important to keep things in perspective and not let small issues turn into bigger ones.

- **Perfectionism**: Many parents feel pressure to be perfect and may become overly critical of themselves or their children. Indulging in this type of negative thinking can result in emotions of inadequacy and low self-esteem. It's recommended to concentrate on progress rather than perfection and acknowledge small victories along the way to build self-confidence.

- **Personalizing**: This type of negative thinking involves taking things personally and feeling like everything is a reflection of your worth. As a parent, it's easy to take your children's behavior or actions personally, but it's important to remember that their behavior is not usually a reflection of your worth as a parent.

- **Polarizing**: This involves thinking in black-and-white terms and not considering the gray areas. What does that statement mean? This might involve thinking that you are either a good parent or a bad parent without considering the many complexities of parenting. It's important to recognize that parenting is a journey with ups and downs, and there will be both good and bad days.

- **Saying you "should" do something**: This type of negative thinking involves putting pressure on yourself to do things a certain way or meet certain expectations. It's important to remember that there is no one right way to parent and to give yourself grace and flexibility.

Step Two: Remove These Thoughts From Your Mind

When it comes to parenting, negative self-talk can be particularly harmful. Many parents fall into the trap of believing certain negative statements about themselves and their parenting abilities. Here are some common negative self-talk statements you might make and why you should remove them from your thinking:

- **My kids hate me**: This type of negative self-talk can be particularly harmful to both you and your children. Believing that your children hate you can lead to feelings of guilt, shame, and even depression. It can also make you more likely to react poorly to your children's behavior, further exacerbating the problem. Instead of believing this statement, try to focus on the positive aspects of your relationship with your children and look for ways to improve it.

- **I'm doing a bad job**: This type of negative thinking can be particularly insidious, as it can become a self-fulfilling prophecy. If you believe that you are doing a bad job as a parent, you may be more likely to make mistakes or react poorly to your children's behavior. Instead of focusing on your mistakes, try to focus on your successes as a parent, no matter how small they may seem.

- **I'm messing up my kid**: Parenting is a challenging job, and it's natural to worry that you may be doing something wrong. However, constantly worrying about whether or not you're messing up your child can be harmful to both you and your child.

- **I'm just like my parents**: Many parents worry that they will repeat the same mistakes their own parents made. However, it's important to remember that you are not your parents, and you have the power to make different choices. Instead of focusing on the negative aspects of your own upbringing, try to focus on the positive things you learned from your parents.

- **I'll never be as good a parent as "X"**: Comparing yourself to other parents can be harmful and counterproductive. Instead of focusing on what other parents are doing, try to focus on your own strengths and abilities as a parent.

- **This will never end**: Parenting can be exhausting and overwhelming at times, and it's natural to feel like you're never going to get a break. However, it's important to remember that parenting is a journey, and there will be ups and downs along the way. Instead of focusing on the negative aspects of your situation, try to focus on the positive things you can do to make things better.

By recognizing and removing these types of negative thoughts from your mind, you may become a more confident and effective parent. You must have a positive attitude and a willingness to learn and grow so that you may become the best parent you can be.

Step Three: Focus on the Positive

Parents can effectively manage their anger and enhance their general well-being by using positive self-talk. Here are some methods to implement positive self-talk:

- **Treat yourself like you would a friend**: Many parents are too hard on themselves and criticize their actions and decisions constantly. Instead, consider approaching yourself with the same kindness, support, and encouragement you would offer to a friend.

- **Remember self-care**: It's essential to take care of your physical, emotional, and mental well-being. When you prioritize self-care, you are better equipped to handle stressful situations and negative self-talk.

- **Limit exposure to negativity**: Limiting exposure to negativity means avoiding people or situations that bring you down. This can include negative self-talk or other people's negative comments or behaviors.

- **Practice gratitude**: Practicing gratitude involves recognizing and being thankful for the positive things in your life. Shifting your focus to the positive aspects can assist in changing negative self-talk into a more constructive outlook.

- **Post positive affirmations**: Put down encouraging messages and display them in prominent locations, like your office or bathroom mirror. Reading these affirmations daily can help reinforce positive self-talk.

- **Find humor**: Laughter is an excellent way to combat negative self-talk. Play a funny podcast, watch a funny movie, or read a funny book.

- **Create psychological distance from yourself**: Sometimes, it's helpful to create psychological distance from negative thoughts by imagining them as objects or characters separate from yourself. This technique can help you distance yourself from negative self-talk and reframe your thoughts.

- **If needed, work with a professional**: If negative self-talk is impacting your mental health, seek help from a mental health professional. A therapist can provide guidance and support to help you develop positive self-talk skills.

Practicing positive self-talk is an effective way for parents to manage their anger and improve their overall well-being. By focusing on the positive and adopting healthy habits, parents can cultivate a more positive and supportive inner voice.

Story

At some point, one father enrolled in a parenting class I was leading, and he kept sharing his negative complaints with me from the very first session.

"I'm just a bad dad."; "I can't get anything right with my kids."; and so on.

At first, I tried to reassure him and offer suggestions for improving his relationship with his children, but it seemed like no matter what I said, he couldn't shake his negative self-talk.

It didn't take long for me to realize that the father's own negative self-talk was the big culprit in his angry outbursts and strained relationship with his kids. Because he felt inadequate, he would lash out at his children, creating a cycle of negativity and frustration.

I knew that we needed to address his negative self-talk if we were going to make any progress in the class. So, I started working with him to find positives in his parenting and in his relationship with his children. We began by acknowledging his strengths as a father, no matter how small they might seem. Even simple things like playing catch with his son or making his daughter laugh were steps in the right direction.

Once he started to see that he was capable of doing good things as a dad, we worked on reframing his negative self-talk. Instead of telling himself that he was a bad father, he began to say things like, "I'm still learning, but I'm trying my best," or "I may make mistakes, but I can always make things right with my kids."

It wasn't easy, and there were setbacks along the way, but gradually, the father's negative self-talk began to fade away. He became more patient with his children, and his relationship with them improved. I saw a noticeable change in him during our sessions, and it was heartening to watch him grow as a father.

In the end, the father learned that he was not a bad dad but rather a dad who was struggling with negative self-talk. By focusing on the positives and changing his inner dialogue, he was able to transform his relationship with his kids and become the father he always wanted to be.

Let the Work Begin: Challenging My Negative Thoughts Worksheet

Here is an exercise to take the reins into your own hands and lead negative thoughts off your mind!

Instructions

- Get a plan paper and answer these questions on it.
- Find a negative thought that you commonly experience.
- To combat the negative thought, pose the following questions to yourself.

Challenging Questions

- Is this thought true?
- What evidence do I have to support this thought?
- Is this thought helpful to me?

- Am I jumping to conclusions?
- Am I taking things too personally?
- What would I say to a friend who had this thought?
- Which scenario would be the worst?
- What is the best thing that could happen?
- What is the most likely outcome?
- How important will this be in a year? 5 years?

Additional Notes

- It's important to be honest with yourself when answering these challenging questions.
- Keep in mind to swap out the negative thinking for one that is uplifting and truthful.
- You can repeat this exercise with different negative thoughts as they come up.

In this chapter, we discussed negative self-talk and its impact on parenting. We highlighted the different types of negative thinking that you should be aware of and provided ways to challenge and replace them with positive self-talk. We also shared a story of a father who struggled with negative self-talk and how he worked to change his thought patterns. The key takeaway from this chapter is that negative self-talk can have a significant impact on parenting, and it's essential to recognize and address it to improve parenting and family relationships. When you practice positive self-talk, limit exposure to negativity, and seek help if needed, you may become more confident and effective in your parenting. In the next chapter, we are going to look at how to effectively communicate matters. This is one important chapter to look out for.

Chapter 5:

Let's Talk—Effective Communication Matters

As a parent, do you ever feel like no matter how nicely you say something to your child, they just don't listen? It's a common experience that can leave you feeling frustrated and unsure of what to do. There is a better method than yelling, even though it may seem like the only alternative. Effective communication with your child is key to establishing and maintaining a healthy relationship. In this chapter, we'll explore the importance of parent-child communication and how it can improve your relationship with your child.

The Importance of Parent-Child Communication

It's crucial for parents to have clear lines of communication with their children. Not only does it help things run more smoothly, but it also strengthens the bond between parent and child. Below are several explanations for why parent-child interaction is important:

Family functions run more smoothly: When you and your children communicate effectively, you can work together to make sure that the household runs smoothly. For example, you can ask your children for help with tasks such as cooking, cleaning, and grocery shopping. Children can feel valued and included in the family's activities, and you can benefit from your children's help and input. This can help to reduce conflict and create a sense of teamwork and togetherness within the family, making life more enjoyable.

It establishes and maintains a relationship between parent and child: Communication is a key component of any relationship, including the relationship between parent and child. When you and your child talk to each other regularly, you can get to know each other better, share your thoughts and feelings, and develop a deeper understanding of each other. This can help to create a strong and lasting bond between parent and child.

The parent-child relationship is strengthened through the feedback from dialogue: When you communicate with your children, you may give each other feedback about your thoughts, feelings, and actions. Regardless of whether the feedback is favorable or unfavorable, it will always serve to strengthen the bond between you and your children. For example, if your child tells you that they appreciate something you did, you will feel valued and appreciated. Similarly, if you tell your child that you are proud of them for achieving something, they will feel supported and encouraged. This can help build a sense of trust and mutual respect between parent and child.

Greatly improves parent-child relationship: When you communicate with your children and talk to each other in a respectful and supportive way, they can build a relationship based on trust, understanding, and love. When your child feels close to you, they are more likely to open up about their struggles and ask for help when they need it. This can prevent small issues from turning into bigger problems and can promote positive behaviors and decision-making.

Builds understanding and trust: Communication is essential in building understanding and trust. When you talk openly and honestly with your children, both parties may develop a better understanding of each other's perspectives, needs, and feelings. This can help to create a sense of trust and security within the family, which is essential for children's healthy development.

The "How To's" of Effective Communication

To effectively communicate with your children, active listening is a crucial skill. It involves giving your full attention to your child and making them feel heard and understood. Active listening is more than just hearing the words your child is saying; It necessitates a deeper level of interaction with them.

The following elements make up active listening:

1. One of the key aspects of active listening is giving your full attention to your child. This means stopping what you're doing and focusing solely on your child's words and actions. When your child knows that you are giving them your undivided attention, they are more likely to open up and share their thoughts and feelings with you.

2. Another crucial component of active listening is eye contact. Eye contact shows your child that you are interested in what they have to say and that you are taking them seriously.

3. Also, it is beneficial to get close to your child. This means crouching down or sitting on the floor with your

child so that you are eye-to-eye. Doing so shows your child that you are fully engaged in the conversation and that their thoughts and feelings matter to you. When you are towering over your child, they may feel intimidated or even ignored, so taking the time to get down on their level can make a big difference in how they perceive your communication. Plus, it can be a great way to connect with your child on a more personal level, and it can help build trust and understanding between you.

4. Reflecting or repeating back what your child is saying is also an essential part of active listening. This involves paraphrasing what your child has said to ensure that you understand their message correctly. It helps to clarify any misunderstandings and lets your child know that you are truly listening to them.

Incorporating active listening into your communication with your child can greatly improve your relationship with them. When your child feels heard and understood, they are more likely to trust you and feel comfortable opening up to you in the future. Active listening also sets an example for your child, showing them how to listen actively and communicate effectively with others.

Tips for Talking to Your Child

Effective communication with your child is essential for building a strong parent-child relationship. Here are some tips for talking to your child that can help you establish a healthy and open dialogue.

- **Speak in a positive tone**: The tone of your voice can have a significant impact on how your child perceives your message. Speaking in a positive and encouraging tone can help your child feel more receptive and engaged in the conversation. Using a positive tone also shows your child that you respect them and value their thoughts and feelings.

- **Use praise**: Praise is important because kids thrive on encouragement and acknowledgment. Praising your child for their achievements, even small ones, can help build their confidence and self-esteem. This positive reinforcement can also help motivate your child to continue making progress and trying new things.

- **Schedule daily conversational time with them**: Creating dedicated time each day to talk to your child can help establish a routine for open communication. This can be during meals, while driving, or before bedtime. Setting aside time shows your child that you value their thoughts and that they are a priority to you.

- **Be open to talking about all sorts of feelings**: Establishing a secure environment where your child may express their emotions without fear of criticism or retaliation is crucial. When your child knows they can express themselves freely, they are more likely to communicate openly and honestly with you.

- **Talk about relatable topics**: Choosing topics that are relatable to your child can help keep them engaged and interested in the conversation. Discussing topics that your child is familiar with, such as their interests or hobbies, can also help establish common ground and build rapport.

- **Ask for their help or advice**: Asking your child for their help or advice on a task or problem can show them that their input is valued and appreciated. This may encourage critical thinking and problem-solving skills in your child.

- **Ask open-ended questions**: A more in-depth dialogue can be facilitated by posing open-ended questions that call for more information than a simple "yes" or "no" response. Open-ended questions can also help your child express their thoughts and feelings more clearly.

- **Express lots of interest**: Showing a genuine interest in your child's thoughts, ideas, and activities can help create a strong parent-child relationship. Taking an active interest in your child's life can also help establish trust and improve communication.

Effective communication with your child is critical for building a strong and healthy relationship. Using these tips for talking to your child can help establish a safe and open dialogue that allows for honest and meaningful conversations.

Getting Your Children to Listen... Without You Yelling

As parents, we've all been there—our children are not listening to us, and we feel like we're at our wits' end. It's easy to let our frustration boil over and resort to yelling, but there are better ways to get our children to listen. Here are some tips to help you get your children to listen without losing your cool:

- **Stay calm**: It's important to stay calm when trying to get your children to listen. When you're upset or agitated, take a moment to breathe and think before you say a word. When you stay calm, you model for your child how to handle their emotions and it can also help de-escalate a tense situation.

- **Remove the word "don't"**: Instead of telling your child what not to do, tell them what you want them to do. For example, instead of saying "don't run," say "please walk." This puts a positive spin on your request and is more likely to get your child to listen.

- **Say thank you in advance**: When making a request, say "thank you" in advance. For example, "Thank you for putting away your toys before dinner." This shows that you have confidence in your child's ability to follow through and can be motivating for them.

- **Give one warning**: If your child is not following the rules, give them one warning before following through with a consequence. Make sure they understand what the consequence will be if they don't comply.

- **Follow through with a consequence**: If your child does not follow the rules after one warning, it's important to follow through with a consequence. Be consistent with the consequences and make sure they are appropriate for the behavior. For example, if your child refuses to clean their room, taking away screen time for the day may be an appropriate consequence.

- **Be consistent**: To encourage your kids to listen, consistency is essential. Check to see that you're consistently applying the laws and implementing the appropriate penalties as necessary. This helps your child understand what is expected of them and what the consequences will be if they don't comply.

By following these tips, you can help your children listen to you without resorting to yelling. Remember, it takes time and patience to build good listening habits in your children, but with practice and consistency, you can make progress.

Story

One mother once approached me about her anger issues. Let's call her Sarah, came to me for help, feeling frustrated and helpless. She shared that she had been yelling at her children frequently because they didn't listen to her when she asked them to do something. She said she had tried everything, from nagging to pleading, but nothing seemed to work until she resorted to yelling.

I listened to Sarah carefully and then introduced her to some strategies that could help her communicate more effectively with her children. We started with active listening, which meant giving her full attention to her children when they talked to her and getting down to their level so that she could connect with them emotionally. We then worked on improving her tone of voice and using positive language when communicating with her children.

One of the most important things that Sarah learned was to remove the word "don't" from her vocabulary. Instead of saying, "Don't jump on the bed," she would say, "Please get off the bed and play somewhere else." We also practiced saying "Thank you in advance" to encourage her children to comply with her requests.

Another strategy we worked on was giving one warning before following through with a consequence. This helped her children understand that their actions had consequences, and they were more likely to listen to her requests.

With consistent practice and patience, Sarah was able to change her approach to communicating with her children. She was shocked to find that it was much simpler to convince her kids to listen without shouting. She reported feeling much more connected with her children and enjoying a more peaceful and positive relationship with them.

Sarah's story is a great example of how simple changes in our communication style can make a huge difference in our relationships with our children. It takes practice and patience, but with the right strategies and support, it is possible to improve our communication and build better relationships with our children.

Let the Work Begin: The No Yelling Challenge

Congratulations on taking the first step toward improving your communication with your children! Yelling is a common problem that many parents struggle with, but it's never too late to change.

The *No Yelling Challenge* is designed to help you break the habit of yelling and find more effective ways to communicate with your children. This challenge will last for seven days, and each day you will focus on a different aspect of your communication with your child.

Day 1: Take a deep breath.

Today, whenever you feel the urge to yell, take a deep breath and count to 10 before responding to your child. Doing this will help you keep your composure and not lose your cool.

Day 2: Use positive language.

Try to use positive language instead of negative language when talking to your child. Instead of saying, "Stop running in the house," say, "Please walk in the house." This helps to keep the conversation positive and encourages good behavior.

Day 3: Show appreciation.

Take time to appreciate your child's positive behaviors. If your child does something you like, say, "Thank you for doing that," or "I appreciate it when you do that." This reinforces positive behaviors and encourages more of them.

Day 4: Listen actively.

Take time to actively listen to your child. When your child is speaking, give them your full attention, make eye contact, and reflect back on what they're saying to make sure you understand. This demonstrates to your child how much you regard their ideas and emotions.

Day 5: Offer choices.

Wherever feasible, provide your child with options. This helps to give them a sense of control and can reduce power struggles.

For example, instead of saying, "Put your shoes on," say, "Do you want to put your shoes on by yourself, or do you want me to help you?"

Day 6: Set boundaries.

Set clear boundaries for your child's behavior and stick to them. When your child misbehaves, calmly remind them of the boundary and the consequences for crossing it. This helps to establish clear expectations and encourages good behavior.

Day 7: Celebrate your success.

At the end of the day, take time to reflect on your successes. Celebrate the moments when you were able to stay calm and communicate effectively with your child. This helps to reinforce positive behaviors and encourages you to continue improving your communication with your child.

Congratulations on completing the *No Yelling Challenge*! Remember, effective communication takes practice and patience, but it's worth it in the end. Keep up the good work!

Effective communication with children involves active listening, speaking in a positive tone, setting aside time each day to talk, being open to talking about all sorts of feelings, talking about relatable topics, asking for their help or advice, asking open-ended questions, and expressing interest. When trying to get children to listen without yelling, it is important to stay calm, remove negative language, say thank you in advance, give one warning, follow through with a consequence, and be consistent. In the next chapter, we will focus on how to lead with love and discipline your children in a positive way.

Chapter 6:

Leading with Love—Positive Parenting

Is positive parenting just a trendy buzzword, or does it actually have merit in raising happy, healthy children? Can a parenting philosophy that emphasizes love and empathy really be effective in disciplining children and shaping their behavior?

When I first heard about positive parenting, I have to admit that I was a bit skeptical. I pictured a bunch of parents sitting around in a circle, more like hippies sitting around in a circle, holding hands and singing "Kumbaya," chanting positive affirmations and ignoring their children's bad behavior. Was that all there was, I wondered. Yet, let me reassure you that it is not about being a pushover or allowing your children to act out without supervision.

Positive parenting is a philosophy that focuses on building strong, healthy relationships between parents and children, while also setting clear boundaries and expectations. It's about leading with love, respect, and empathy, instead of relying on fear, punishment, or control. Because let's face it, being a parent is already a difficult job. It's natural to feel overwhelmed, frustrated, or even angry at times. But the good news is that positive parenting can help you navigate these challenges with grace and compassion. Whether you are a seasoned parent or a new one, there is always something new to learn about positive parenting, and this chapter will give you the tools you need to build a stronger and more positive relationship with your child. If you are ready to learn more about this approach and how to put it into practice, let's get to it!

Positive Parenting Explained

Positive parenting is a parenting style that focuses on building a deep connection between you and your child while avoiding harsh punishment.

Qualities of Positive Parenting

On second thought, positive parenting is more than just a parenting style—it's a way of life. It's about nurturing your child's emotional, social, and cognitive development while fostering a positive relationship built on mutual trust and respect. One of the cornerstones of positive parenting is the use of positive reinforcement to encourage good behavior and help children learn from their mistakes. In this section, we'll discuss some of the key qualities of positive parenting, such as its focus on situations you can control.

Here are some key features of positive parenting:

Focuses on building a deep connection between parent and child

One of the main goals of positive parenting is to build a deep connection between you and your child. This connection is built through a focus on communication, trust, and empathy. Positive parents listen to their children, respect their opinions, and work to understand their feelings. By doing so, you create a safe and supportive environment where your children feel heard and loved.

Doesn't use harsh punishment

Instead of punishing your children for their mistakes, positive parents focus on helping them learn from their mistakes. This entails directing their attention in a more positive direction through problem-solving, redirection, and natural consequences.

Tries to "catch kids being good"

Positive parenting also focuses on "catching kids being good." Instead of just correcting bad behavior, you make an effort to notice and praise their positive behavior. This helps them build self-esteem, confidence, and a positive self-image.

Uses Praise

Praise is a key tool in positive parenting. You should use praise to reinforce positive behavior and to build your children's confidence. Praise should be specific and genuine, focusing on effort and progress rather than just results.

Focuses on What You Can Control

Positive parents focus on what you can control, which is your own behavior and reactions. Understanding that you cannot control your children's behavior, but you can control how you respond to it. This lessens frustrations if reality doesn't turn out as you expected. Focusing on what you can control also enables you to acknowledge that your children are their own people. This means they are capable of making their own decisions which may be good or bad. By modeling positive behavior and your reactions, you are creating a positive environment that encourages good behavior in your children.

How Can I Implement Positive Parenting?

When it comes to implementing positive parenting in your own home, it can be overwhelming to know where to start. But don't worry; with a few simple strategies, you can begin to shift your parenting style toward a more positive approach. In this section, we'll explore some practical tips and techniques for incorporating positive parenting into your everyday routine. From establishing household rules to showing affection, these strategies will help you build a strong, positive relationship with your child while setting the foundation for their future success. Let's get started!

Establish Rules and Discuss Them Often

Establishing clear and consistent rules is an essential part of positive parenting. By doing so, you may create a structured environment that helps your children understand what is expected of them. You should sit down with your children and collaboratively develop rules that are age-appropriate and consistent with family values. It is important to discuss these rules regularly and adjust them, as necessary.

Reward or Reinforce Good Behavior

A potent tool for good parenting is positive reinforcement. Rather than focusing on the negative behavior, you should reward your children for being good. This can take many forms, such as verbal praise, hugs, or rewards like stickers, extra playtime, or gifts. By reinforcing good behavior, you may encourage their children to continue behaving positively.

Be Consistent

Consistency is key to positive parenting. Children thrive in predictable environments, and inconsistent parenting can lead to confusion and anxiety. You should strive to be consistent in your rules and expectations, as well as your responses to your children's behavior. This consistency will help them feel safe, secure, and confident in their environment.

Focus on Affection

Showing affection is crucial in positive parenting. Your children may feel more loved and supported if you show them your affection by hugging them, saying encouraging things, and spending quality time with them. Children who receive regular affection from their parents are more likely to develop healthy emotional regulation skills and positive self-esteem.

Discipline in Positive Parenting

When it comes to parenting, discipline is often a hot topic. It's important to set boundaries and teach children right from wrong, but traditional forms of discipline, such as spanking or yelling, can be counterproductive and even harmful. Positive discipline is an alternative approach that focuses on guiding children through difficult behaviors rather than punishing them.

A Definition of Positive Discipline

Positive discipline is a method of guiding children's behavior that focuses on teaching rather than punishing. It helps children develop self-discipline and learn how to make positive choices. Positive discipline emphasizes the importance of building a strong relationship between you and your child and emphasizes respectful communication. What does positive discipline encompass?

Focuses on Giving Direction Rather than Punishing

Positive discipline focuses on helping your children understand the consequences of their behavior and encouraging them to make positive choices. Rather than using punishment to deter negative behavior, positive discipline emphasizes the importance of teaching children how to manage their emotions and behavior.

States "Connection Must Come Before Correction"

Positive discipline emphasizes the importance of building a strong relationship between you and your child. When your child feels connected to you, they are more likely to listen and cooperate. Positive discipline encourages parents to build connections with their children through active listening, positive communication, and spending quality time together.

Is Respectful and Encouraging

Positive discipline is rooted in respect and encouragement toward children. Rather than focusing on punishment, it emphasizes positive reinforcement and acknowledging good behavior. This approach recognizes the importance of understanding and validating children's emotions while also encouraging them to develop empathy toward others. By creating a supportive and respectful environment, positive discipline helps children build their self-esteem, foster a sense of responsibility and accountability, and strengthen their relationships with parents and caregivers.

What It Teaches Our Children

Good discipline is more than simply correcting undesirable actions. It's a way of teaching children how to navigate the world and grow into responsible, self-disciplined, and confident adults. Here are some of the key qualities that positive discipline can teach our children:

- **Responsibility**: Children who get positive discipline learn to accept accountability for their behaviors and decisions. Rather than blaming others for their mistakes, they learn to accept the consequences of their actions and make things right when they've done something wrong.

- **Self-discipline**: Children learn how to control their own conduct through constructive discipline, which establishes clear expectations and boundaries.. They learn to make good choices even when it's hard and to resist temptation and delay gratification.

- **Good behavior**: Positive discipline emphasizes positive reinforcement, so children learn that good behaviors are rewarded with praise and attention. They're more likely to repeat those behaviors in the future, creating a cycle of positive behavior and positive reinforcement.

- **Self-esteem**: Positive discipline helps children develop a strong sense of self-worth and self-esteem. By emphasizing their strengths and acknowledging their efforts, children learn to believe in themselves and their abilities.

- **Healthy ways of dealing with stress**: Positive discipline teaches children coping mechanisms and healthy ways to deal with stress. They learn to identify and express their emotions and to seek support when they need it.

Incorporating positive discipline into your parenting approach takes time and effort, but the benefits are worth it. By focusing on teaching rather than punishing, you can help your children develop the skills they need to thrive in the world.

Key Features of Positive Discipline to Implement

A successful and kind method of behavior management for children is positive discipline. It focuses on the long-term goals of raising confident, responsible, and compassionate individuals. Here are some key parts of positive discipline that you can implement in your parenting approach.

- **Never using physical punishment**: Physical punishment is not only ineffective but also harmful to children. It can lead to anxiety, depression, aggression, and lower academic achievement. Positive discipline avoids physical punishment and focuses on building a strong emotional connection with your child.

- **Showing and telling (modeling behavior)**: Children learn by observing their parents and other role models. Positive discipline involves modeling the behavior you want your child to exhibit, such as using kind words, being patient, and showing respect. You can also explain the reasons behind your actions and involve your child in decision-making.

- **Setting effective consequences**: Positive discipline emphasizes natural and logical consequences instead of punishment. This implies that the punishment must be fitting for the behavior and aid in your child's growth. Effective consequences are also respectful, consistent, and given with empathy.

- **Listening to your child**: One of the essential parts of positive discipline is active listening. This means giving your child your full attention, acknowledging their feelings, and validating their experiences. This may enhance their problem-solving skills and ability to trust and communicate with others.

- **Preparing for outbursts and knowing how to deal with them**: Children frequently have tantrums and meltdowns.. Positive discipline involves anticipating triggers, recognizing the signs of stress, and having a plan to de-escalate the situation. This can include taking a break, using calming techniques, and validating your child's feelings.

- **Focusing on what you want them to do rather than what you don't want them to do**: Positive discipline encourages positive behavior by focusing on what you want your child to do rather than what you don't want them to do. For example, instead of saying, "Stop running," you can say, "Walk slowly." This helps your child understand the desired behavior and reinforces it positively.

- **Removing "no" from vocabulary**: Overusing the word "no" can lead to power struggles and defiance. Positive discipline suggests replacing "no" with more positive alternatives such as "Let's find another way" or "How about we do this instead."

- **Playing with them**: Play is a natural and fun way to connect with your child and teach them social skills. Positive discipline involves playing with your child regularly, following their lead, and encouraging creativity and imagination.

- **Using positive time-outs**: Positive time-outs are a non-punitive way to help your child calm down, reflect on their behavior, and learn self-regulation skills. They involve giving your child a safe and comfortable space to take a break and offering support and validation.

By implementing these key parts of positive discipline, you can create a nurturing and supportive environment that helps your child thrive. Although it requires patience, persistence, and time, the benefits are worthwhile.

Story

I had a client named Mark in one of my parenting classes. Mark was a father of two and had a reputation for being a no-nonsense, tough-love parent. He was always the first to raise his voice and never shied away from using physical punishment to discipline his children. Mark's wife, Sofi, was the one who enrolled them in the class. She was concerned about their children's behavior and was hoping to find a better way to parent them.

In the beginning, Mark was resistant to the idea of positive parenting. He believed that it was for weak, fragile people and that the modern world was trying to go soft on children. He preferred scolding and physical punishment, thinking that was the only way to learn from one's behavior. It took him a long time to understand the tenets of positive parenting and get on board with the program.

But one day, during a class discussion, I asked Mark if he learned better when he was shown encouragement or when he was told he was wrong. He paused for a moment and thought about it. He realized that he responded better to positive reinforcement and that his children were no different. Slowly but surely, Mark started implementing the principles of positive parenting. He stopped using physical punishment and instead focused on showing and telling his children how to behave. He started setting effective consequences, listening to his children, and preparing for outbursts.

It wasn't an easy journey for Mark, and there were times when he struggled to maintain his composure. But with each passing day, he found that he was becoming a better parent. He felt closer to his children, and they felt closer to him. He began to see the positive effects of his parenting as his children became more responsible, self-disciplined, and confident.

Looking back, Mark now realizes that positive parenting is not about being weak or going soft on your children. It's about having the fortitude to treat your kids with love and respect, even under trying circumstances. Teaching kids to be responsible, courteous, and compassionate people is the goal. Mark is grateful that he took the chance to try something new and that he now has a better relationship with his children than he ever thought possible.

Let the Work Begin: Charts Galore!

Now that you have learned about the key principles of positive discipline, it's time to put them into practice. One effective tool for reinforcing good behavior is using behavior charts. With behavior charts, you can track progress and give rewards for positive behaviors.

To create your own behavior charts, start by identifying the behaviors you want to reinforce. This could be anything from doing homework on time to cleaning up toys after playing. Once you have identified the behaviors, decide on the rewards you will give for good behavior. Examples of rewards may be an extra allowance or the chance to invite a friend over for a playdate.

After creating the behavior chart, it's important to go over it with your child and discuss how it functions, as well as the positive outcomes for displaying good behavior. Encourage your child to participate in creating the chart and choosing their own rewards.

It's important to remember that behavior charts should be used as a positive reinforcement tool, not a punishment system. Be consistent with using the chart and give praise and rewards for good behavior.

If you find that your child is not responding to the chart, it may be time to reevaluate the chart and adjust it accordingly. Remember, every child is different, and what works for one may not work for another.

You may promote good conduct in your child and reinforce the ideas of positive discipline by making and using behavior charts.. So, let the work begin and start creating your own behavior charts today!

In this chapter, we discussed the importance of building a strong, healthy relationship with your child by using positive discipline techniques. We covered key aspects of positive parenting, including respect and encouragement, teaching responsibility, self-discipline, good behaviors, and self-esteem, as well as how to deal with stress in healthy ways. We also explored the key parts of positive discipline to implement, including never using physical punishment, showing and telling, setting effective consequences, listening to your child, preparing for outbursts, focusing on what you want them to do, removing "no" from vocabulary, playing with them, and using positive time-outs.

In the interactive element, we provided resources for creating behavior charts and encouraged readers to customize them to fit their family's specific needs. By implementing positive discipline techniques and consistently reinforcing good behavior, parents can foster a healthy, respectful relationship with their children.

Moving forward, in the next chapter, we will explore the importance of self-care for parents and caregivers. We will discuss the physical and emotional toll of parenting and provide practical tips for self-care and stress management. By taking care of ourselves, we can better care for our children and maintain a healthy, balanced family dynamic.

Chapter 7:

You Too Need a Break—The Importance of Self-Care

Does wanting time away from my kids make me a bad parent? Does it make me a selfish parent if I spend my time away from my kids?

Prioritizing your well-being allows you to take better care of your child and create a happier, healthier family dynamic. In this chapter, we'll explore the importance of self-care for your parenting role and provide you with some practical tips on how to make it a part of your daily routine. You will discover ways to fit it into your busy schedule and even get ideas on how to take a break when you can't physically leave your home. We will also explore why accepting self-care without feeling guilty is necessary for your mental and emotional health.

You Gotta Get Rid of the Guilt

As a parent, you may have heard the phrase "self-care" thrown around a lot. But what exactly is self-care, and why is it important for you? Engaging in self-care activities can help reduce stress, improve energy levels, and provide a sense of balance in your life. This can have a direct impact on your mental health and emotional well-being, including reducing anger.

It can be easy to feel like you need to be there for your child all of the time. Society has created this false narrative that good parents want to spend every moment with their children and that any desire for alone time is selfish. It's common for parents to experience feelings of guilt when they take time for themselves, even if they truly require that break. However, it is important for everyone, including parents, to have time for themselves.

When you believe you are not providing enough for your child, you may feel terrible about having time for yourself. This negative self-talk can be dangerous and is in no way beneficial. In fact, taking time for yourself can make you a better parent by allowing you to recharge and be more present when you are with your child.

Remember that everyone needs time to themselves, even parents. Whether you are an introvert who needs alone time to recharge or just need a break from the constant demands of parenthood, it is okay to take time for yourself. It can even help you create a better relationship with your child by allowing you to be more present and patient when you are together.

By taking the time to care for yourself, you are better equipped to handle the challenges of parenting and other responsibilities. Self-care can help you manage your emotions and prevent burnout, which can, in turn, reduce the likelihood of becoming reactive and angry in situations.

"What are some ways that you can take time for yourself without feeling bad about it? One option is to schedule regular alone time, whether it is a daily walk or weekly date night. It can also be helpful to communicate with your partner or support system about your need for alone time and work together to make it happen. And if you can't physically get away, finding ways to create alone time at home, such as reading a book or taking a bath, can still be beneficial.

It's important to prioritize self-care and not feel guilty about it. Remember, self-care isn't selfish; it's necessary. Taking the time to care for yourself can actually benefit both you and your child in the long run.

Self-Care Tips for Moms and Dads

Practicing self-care is a crucial part of your parenting journey. In addition to reducing anger, self-care has numerous advantages for individuals. There are several other advantages to practicing self-care that should be noted:

- **Reduces stress**: Self-care routines may assist in lowering stress levels. When you take the time to care for yourself, you are able to recharge and replenish your energy, which can help you to handle stress better.

- **Improves physical health**: Self-care activities such as exercise, getting enough sleep, and eating healthy foods can all contribute to better physical health. When you take care of your physical health, you are better able to tackle the demands of parenting and daily life.

- **Boosts mental health**: Moreover, self-care might improve your mental wellness. Taking time for yourself can help to reduce feelings of anxiety and depression and can improve overall mood and emotional well-being.

- **Increases productivity**: When you practice self-care regularly, you are better able to focus and be productive in other areas of your life. By taking the time to care for yourself, you are able to recharge and come back to your responsibilities with a renewed sense of energy and focus.

- **Enhances relationships**: Practicing self-care can also help to enhance your relationships with others. When you feel good about yourself and are taking care of your own needs, you are better able to show up for the people in your life and form stronger, more meaningful connections.

Practicing self-care is essential for maintaining overall health and well-being. It helps reduce anger, stress, and other negative emotions.

Forms of Self-Care

Self-care contributes to improved physical and mental health, increased productivity, and stronger relationships with others, but one form of self-care transforms its corresponding aspect of your life.

- **Physical self-care**: This form of self-care emphasizes your physical wellness. It includes activities such as eating well, getting enough sleep, exercising, and taking care of any physical health concerns you may have. Many parents neglect physical self-care because they are busy taking care of their children's needs.

- **Emotional self-care**: You can take care of your emotional well-being through activities such as practicing self-compassion, setting boundaries, and engaging in activities that bring you joy. Emotional self-care is important for your parenting journey because you may put your own emotional needs on hold in order to take care of your children.

- **Social self-care**: This form of self-care helps you nurture your relationships with others. It involves activities such as spending time with friends and family, engaging in activities you enjoy with others, and joining social groups. Social self-care is crucial for parents because it can be isolating to care for children without a functional support system.

- **Mental self-care**: This is the kind of self-care that keeps you sane! It includes activities such as practicing mindfulness, seeking therapy or counseling, and engaging in activities that challenge your mind. Mental self-care is a parenting essential because caring for children can be mentally draining and stressful.

- **Spiritual self-care**: A connection between your spiritual activities and beliefs is made via spiritual self-care. Prayer, meditation, and attending worship are a few of the things that are included in it. Spiritual self-care can be important for parents who find solace in their spiritual beliefs and practices.

Physical Self-Care

The most frequently ignored component of self-care for parents is taking care of their bodies, which is what physical self-care is all about. Here are some practical ways to practice physical self-care:

- **Exercise**. Exercise on a regular basis is crucial for sustaining both mental and physical well-being. Finding the time to work out while being a parent might be difficult, but it is essential. Exercise can increase sleep quality, energy levels, and stress reduction. You can find ways to incorporate physical activity into your daily routine, such as taking a walk with your child or doing a workout video at home while they nap.

- **Sleep**. Sleep is essential for both physical and mental well-being. Increased stress, anger, and worse cognitive performance can result from sleep deprivation. As a parent, it can be challenging to get enough sleep with the demands of childcare, but it's essential to prioritize rest. You can make an effort to create a sleep-friendly environment, such as reducing noise and light in your bedroom, establishing a consistent bedtime routine, and avoiding screen time before bed.

- **Eat healthily**. Eating a healthy diet is crucial for maintaining physical health and reducing the risk of chronic illnesses. As a parent, it can be tempting to rely on fast food or quick snacks, but making an effort to eat a balanced diet is essential. You can try meal prepping or planning healthy meals in advance, which can save time and make it easier to eat well.

- **Get a massage**. Massage is an excellent way to relieve stress and promote physical relaxation. A professional massage may be out of reach for some parents, but you can consider asking a partner or friend for a massage or trying self-massage techniques.

- **Cuddle.** Physical touch and closeness with loved ones can be incredibly comforting and promote relaxation. Cuddling with your partner or child can be an excellent way to practice physical self-care.

- **Take a hot shower.** Relaxation and muscular pain relief may both be helped by taking a hot shower. Taking a few minutes to enjoy a hot shower may be a simple but effective way to practice physical self-care.

- **Drink chamomile tea or warm milk.** Chamomile tea and warm milk are both known for their relaxation-promoting properties. Drinking a warm, calming beverage before bed can help promote restful sleep and relaxation.

Remember that physical self-care is critical for maintaining physical and mental health as a parent. By incorporating these activities into your routine, you can prioritize taking care of your body and promote overall wellness.

Emotional Self-Care

The importance of emotional self-care is equal to that of physical self-care. It's essential to pay attention to your emotional needs, which can sometimes be ignored in the busyness of parenting. Below are some tips for emotional self-care:

- **Spend time alone.** Everyone requires some alone time to unwind and refuel. Take a break from your daily routine and spend some time doing something you enjoy, such as reading a book, taking a walk, or watching a movie. It's essential to have some time to yourself to reduce stress and maintain a healthy emotional balance.

- **Do things that make you happy.** Engage in activities that bring you joy, whether it's gardening, cooking, dancing, or painting. Schedule time to engage in activities that will make you feel fulfilled and pleased. It's a great way to connect with yourself and improve your overall well-being.

- **Allow yourself to cry.** It's okay to feel sad or overwhelmed at times, and it's essential to allow yourself to cry if you need to. A healthy method to let feelings out and decompress is by crying. Don't feel ashamed or guilty for crying; instead, embrace your emotions and take care of yourself.

- **Laugh**! A fantastic approach to reduce stress and improve your mood is by laughing. Watch a comedy show, spend time with friends who make you laugh, or find something that makes you smile. Laughing helps to reduce cortisol levels, the hormone associated with stress, and can have a positive impact on your overall emotional health.

- **Say no to extra responsibilities.** It's important to set boundaries and say no to extra responsibilities that you can't handle. It's important not to take on too many obligations and to ensure that you're focusing your time and energy on the things that matter most to you. Saying no is a way to take care of yourself and ensure that you have enough time and energy to meet your own needs.

Remember that emotional self-care is unique to each individual. It's essential to find what works for you and what makes you feel good. Don't be afraid to experiment with different activities and approaches until you find the ones that work best for you.

Social Self-Care

Social self-care is essential for parents as it can help to reduce feelings of isolation and loneliness. These are a few strategies for social self-care:

- **Spend time with friends**. Make an effort to schedule time with friends, even if it's just a quick catch-up call or text message. Having a support system of friends who understand what you're going through can be helpful and uplifting.

- **Be creative about social activities you can work around your child's needs**. It can be challenging to find time for socializing when you have children, but it's important to make it a priority. Look for creative ways to socialize that work with your child's schedule. For example, you could have a playdate with other parents and their kids or invite friends over for a meal after your child goes to bed.

- **Plan daily conversational time with adults**. It's simple for you to become engrossed in the everyday tasks of parenting and neglect to socialize with other adults. Set aside some time every day, even for a short while, to interact with other adults.

- **Go on date nights with your partner.** If you have a partner, make it a priority to have regular date nights. This time together can help to strengthen your relationship and provide a much-needed break from parenting.

- **Say no to extra responsibilities.** It's important to set boundaries and prioritize your own needs. Don't feel guilty about saying no to extra responsibilities if it means sacrificing your own well-being. It's okay to put yourself first sometimes.

By practicing social self-care, parents can build supportive relationships, reduce stress and feelings of isolation, and maintain a healthy work-life balance.

Spiritual self-care

Activities that foster inner tranquility, introspection, and a sense of connection to the outside world are all part of spiritual self-care. It is more about making a connection to something significant and bigger than oneself than it is particularly about religious behaviors. Here are some suggestions for engaging in spiritual self-care:

- **Participate in religious services.** If you are religious, attending regular services can be a great way to feel more connected to your community and to a higher power. Even if you can't attend in-person services, many religious organizations offer online services that you can participate in from home.

- **Meditate or pray regularly.** Meditation and prayer can be a great way to quiet your mind, reduce stress, and connect with your inner self. It can be challenging to find time to meditate or pray when you have young children, but even a few minutes a day can make a difference.

- **Do volunteer work.** Helping others can be a great way to connect with your community and feel a sense of purpose. Look for volunteer opportunities that align with your interests and values.

- **Spend time outside.** Being in nature can help you feel more anchored and in touch with the world around you. A quick stroll outside may be energizing and restorative.

- **Reflect on your new life.** Becoming a parent can be a transformative experience. It's okay to reflect on it and the ways it has influenced you. You may find that you have a newfound sense of purpose or that you have developed new values or priorities.

- **Be open to inspiration and awe.** Look for moments of beauty and wonder in your everyday life. It could be as simple as watching a sunset or noticing the way the light filters through the trees. Being open to these moments can help you feel more connected to the world around you.

- **Contribute to causes you believe in.** Supporting causes that are important to you can be a great way to feel more connected to the world and make a positive impact. Whether it's volunteering your time, making a donation, or simply spreading awareness about an issue, every little bit helps.

Story

My wife didn't always yell at our children, but I could spot signs of burnout in her. It was affecting her patience levels, making parenting more challenging than it needed to be. I realized that I was getting more kid-free time than she was, and that was causing her to feel overwhelmed.

So, I encouraged her to make time for herself daily. I suggested that she take an hour here and there to focus on her needs, whether that was exercise, reading, or just taking a relaxing bath. To my surprise, she was grateful for my suggestion and immediately implemented it into her daily routine.

With just a small amount of time each day to focus on her own needs, my wife felt like a brand new person. She had more energy and patience and, overall, felt more positive about life.

Through my work with other parents, I have found that my wife's experience is not uncommon. Parents often neglect their own needs in the midst of raising children, causing them to feel overwhelmed and burned out. But by taking the time to engage in self-care activities, they can reduce their stress levels, improve their mood, and ultimately become better parents.

In working with parents who struggle with anger management, I often use this same approach. I encourage them to find time for themselves each day, even if it's just for a few minutes. Whether it's reading a book, taking a walk, or practicing meditation, these self-care activities can make a world of difference in their lives.

Self-care has a great effect on parents, as I have personally witnessed. They are better able to face the difficulties that come with parenting if they take the time to focus on their own needs. They are more understanding, sympathetic, and patient with their kids..

In conclusion, it's important for parents to make self-care a priority in their lives. By practicing self-care, you may lower their stress levels, lift their spirits, and eventually become better parents. As a parent myself, I know how challenging it can be to find time for self-care, but it's crucial for our own well-being and that of our families.

Let the Work Begin: A Week of Writing It Out

Journaling is a great way to reflect on your thoughts, feelings, and experiences. You can lessen tension and process your emotions with its assistance. Here are seven various diary questions for introspection and self-care:

1. What are the most important things in your life? How do you make sure you include these priorities in your everyday schedule?

2. What is one thing you can do today to take care of yourself? How can you incorporate more self-care into your daily routine?

3. Describe a time when you were pleased with yourself. What did you do to achieve that feeling? How can you replicate that feeling in the future?

4. Write about a time when you felt overwhelmed or stressed. What caused those feelings? What can you do in the future to manage those feelings better?

5. Which activities or objects make you happy? How can you incorporate more of these things into your daily routine?

6. Describe a period in your life when you felt guilty. What caused those feelings? How can you work to let go of that guilt?

7. Write a letter to yourself, telling yourself all the things you need to hear right now. What advice would you give yourself? What kind words would you say to yourself?

8. Take some time each day to reflect on these prompts and write down your thoughts and feelings. Remember, self-care is essential to your well-being, so make it a priority in your daily routine.

Now that you have learned the importance of taking care of yourself and how to incorporate self-care into your routine, let's move on to the next step: Controlling your rage. We all know how easy it is to get angry when we're under stress or feeling overwhelmed, but reacting in anger can have negative consequences on our relationships with our children and overall well-being. In the next chapter, we'll discuss techniques for stopping anger in its tracks, so you can respond calmly and effectively to challenging situations. Let's dive in!

Chapter 8:

In the Heat of the Moment—

Stopping Anger in its Tracks

All of this is great, but what do I do when I feel myself spiraling like I am about to freak out?

Feeling like you're about to explode is a common experience that parents face. Even therapists, who are trained to manage their emotions, have bad days where they feel overwhelmed and out of control. As a parent, it's normal to feel like you're on the brink of losing it, especially when you're overstimulated, frustrated, feeling unappreciated, or experiencing burnout.

Overstimulation can occur when you have too much going on around you, and you feel like you can't keep up. It may happen when you have multiple children who all need your attention at the same time or when your house is noisy and chaotic. Overstimulation can also be caused by external factors, such as loud noises or bright lights.

Frustration is another common reason for feeling like you're going to explode. You may feel frustrated when your child isn't listening to you or when they're misbehaving. Frustration can also arise when you're dealing with a difficult situation, like a sick child or a broken appliance.

Feeling unappreciated is another factor that can contribute to feeling like you're going to explode. When you feel like you're not getting the recognition or support that you need, it's easy to feel overwhelmed and undervalued. This can be particularly challenging for stay-at-home parents, who may not get the same level of acknowledgment and validation that they would in a professional setting.

Burnout is a common issue for parents, especially those who are juggling multiple responsibilities like work, household chores, and childcare. When you're burned out, you may feel exhausted, emotionally drained, and irritable. Burnout can make it difficult to manage your emotions and respond calmly to stressful situations, which can lead to feelings of frustration and overwhelm.

It's important to recognize the signs that you're about to lose it so that you can take steps to manage your emotions before they escalate. In the following sections, we'll explore some strategies for managing anger and preventing meltdowns.

First, Don't Be So Hard On Yourself!

Parenthood can be overwhelming, especially when you feel like you're not doing it right. One of the most important things to remember is that no parent is perfect, and it's okay to make mistakes. In fact, even therapists who specialize in parenting have bad days, as everyone does. It's important to be kind to yourself and not be too hard on yourself.

When you're feeling frustrated or stressed, it can be easy to fall into negative self-talk and criticize yourself. However, this is the worst type of self-criticism because it can lead to feelings of guilt and shame, which are not productive or helpful. Instead, try to focus on the positives and remind yourself that doing your best is what matters.

Additionally, it's essential to remember that parenting is a learning process, and parents are made, not born. It takes time and practice to become a good parent, and it's okay to make mistakes along the way. Making errors might sometimes be a chance for improvement and education.

You may stop being so harsh on yourself as a parent in a number of ways. One option is to give yourself some leeway and admit that being a parent may be challenging, particularly during a crisis. It's reasonable to admit that you don't know everything and to seek assistance when necessary. Another way is to focus on your strengths as a parent rather than your weaknesses. Remember that you are doing your best and that you are a great parent. Finally, try to avoid comparing yourself to other parents as everyone's situation is different, and everyone has their own strengths and weaknesses.

Secondly, Cut Yourself Some Slack

Parenting can be overwhelming at times, and it is important to cut yourself some slack on those tough days. It is crucial to remember that no parent is perfect, and we all have our good and bad moments. It is okay to not have everything under control all the time. When things seem too overwhelming, it is okay to take a step back and take care of yourself. Here are some ways to cut yourself some slack on those challenging parenting days.

- **Take a break and let the kids watch TV for a little while**. This might offer you the respite you need to gather your thoughts and refuel. Remember that it is not the end of the world if your kids watch TV for a bit.

- **Make peace with a messy house.** It is challenging to keep a clean house when you have kids, and it is not worth the added stress to try to maintain a spotless home all the time. Rather than anything else, concentrate on designing a cozy and functional home for your loved ones.

- **Enjoy a glass of wine or your beverage of choice, or indulge in some chocolate**! Sometimes, a little treat can go a long way in lifting your spirits and helping you relax.

- **Use your phone at the playground.** Instead of hovering over your kids while they play, take some time to catch up on your messages, emails, or social media. You deserve a little bit of "me time."

- **Order pizza for dinner.** You don't have to prepare a whole supper every night. Order in or have a simple meal so that you can take a break from cooking and enjoy more quality time with your family.

- **Go to bed early.** Lack of sleep can significantly affect your mood and your ability to cope with stress. It is okay to prioritize sleep and get some extra rest when you need it.

- **Take a walk or spend time outside.** Fresh air and nature can do wonders for your mental health and overall well-being. Take a break and go for a walk or spend some time outdoors with your kids.

- **Hire a babysitter or ask for help.** It is okay to ask for help when you need it. Whether it is hiring a babysitter for a few hours or asking a friend or family member for help with your kids, having someone else to help can give you the break you need to recharge and reset.

- **Treat yourself to something special.** Whether it is a new book, a pedicure, or a night out with friends, it is essential to treat yourself from time to time. Taking the time to do something that you enjoy can help you feel re-energized and ready to take on the challenges of parenting.

- **Practice self-compassion.** Remember to be kind to yourself and give yourself the same grace that you would give to a friend. Acknowledge that parenting is tough, and it is okay to make mistakes and have tough days.

Remember that you are doing the best that you can, and it is okay to take a break and take care of yourself. Try some of these tips to cut yourself some slack and give yourself the time and space you need to recharge and be the best parent that you can be.

Third, Give Yourself a Parent Time-Out

As a parent, it's common to feel like you have to be "on" all the time. However, it's essential to recognize when you need a break and give yourself a parent time-out. A parent time-out is simply stepping away from the situation and taking time for yourself to cool down and recharge. Here are some tips on how to take a parent time-out when emotions are heightened.

First, recognize the signs that you need a time-out. You may feel yourself becoming more irritable, frustrated, or angry. Your heart rate may increase, and your breathing may become shallow. Take a break when you notice these symptoms.

Next, communicate with your child. Let them know that you need a break and that you will be back soon. This not only models healthy coping skills for your child but also gives them a chance to process their emotions as well.

Once you have communicated with your child, find a safe space to take your time out. This could be a separate room in your house or even stepping outside for a few moments. Catch some air, relax, and clear your mind.

During your time-out, it's essential to engage in activities that help you relax and recharge. You can try meditation, listening to music, or practicing yoga. Going for a stroll or performing some light exercise may also be beneficial for you.

It's important to note that a parent time-out isn't a punishment for your child. It's a way to take care of yourself so that you can be a better parent for your child. When you return from your time-out, make sure to check in with your child and continue to communicate with them.

Keep in mind that taking a break when necessary is acceptable. Giving yourself permission to take a time-out can help prevent you from reacting in anger and improve your overall mental health and well-being.

Other ways to give yourself a parent time-out include:

- **Asking for help**: Whether it's asking your partner, a friend, or a family member to help watch your child for a little while, don't be afraid to ask for help.

- **Self-care**: Engage in activities that help you relax and unwind, such as taking a bath, reading a book, or practicing mindfulness.

- **Take a nap**: If you're feeling particularly tired, taking a quick nap can do wonders for your mental state.

- **Step outside your home**: Whether it's going for a walk, hitting the gym, or running errands, a change of environment can often be the rejuvenation your mind and body require.

Giving yourself a parent time-out is an important tool to have in your parenting toolbox. Remember to recognize the signs that you need a break, communicate with your child, and engage in activities that help you relax and recharge. Taking care of yourself is essential to being the best parent you can be.

Finally, Distract Yourself

When you find yourself getting angry or frustrated with your child, one effective way to manage those emotions is to distract yourself. Distractions can help you take your mind off the situation and calm down before you react in anger.

One way to distract yourself is by counting to ten. This technique is often recommended as a way to calm down when you're feeling angry or upset. It gives you time to take a deep breath and refocus your thoughts, which can help prevent you from reacting impulsively.

Another great way to distract yourself is by calling a mom or dad friend. Having a support network of other parents who can relate to your struggles can be incredibly helpful when you're feeling overwhelmed. Just talking to someone who understands can help you feel less alone and more capable of handling whatever challenges come your way.

Doing housework can also be a helpful distraction when you're feeling angry or frustrated. Focusing on a task like washing dishes or folding laundry can be calming and therapeutic, and it can help take your mind off the situation that's causing you stress.

Some other ways to distract yourself include:

- going for a walk or run
- taking a relaxing bath
- doing a craft or hobby that you enjoy
- listening to music or a podcast
- reading a book

It's important to find what works for you and to use these distractions as a way to manage your emotions in a healthy way. By distracting yourself, you can take a step back from the situation and give yourself the space you need to calm down before responding.

In summary, when you're feeling angry or frustrated with your child, distracting yourself can be an effective way to manage those emotions. Whether it's counting to ten, calling a friend, or doing housework, finding healthy ways to distract yourself can help you calm down and prevent you from reacting in anger.

Story

Although I have worked with many parents who struggle with their anger, one dad stands out in my mind. He was making progress with controlling his anger, but there were still times when his children would push his buttons, and he would end up on the verge of exploding.

Despite trying different techniques, like deep breathing or counting to ten, he would still find himself yelling at his children. He frequently felt terrible about this and wondered if he was a lousy dad.

It wasn't until he started practicing parent time-outs and distracting himself that he found a solution. Whenever he felt himself getting angry, he would step away from the situation and take some time to calm down. He would go to his room or go for a walk to cool off.

During his time-outs, he would remind himself of the progress he had made and the techniques he had learned. He would also think about the consequences of his actions if he were to lose his temper. This allowed him to put the situation in a better context and not lose his cool with his kids.

To divert his attention from his rage, he also started doing other things. He found that doing housework or calling a friend could help him calm down and put things in perspective. By the time he returned to his children, he was more relaxed and able to handle the situation without getting angry.

Thanks to his commitment to controlling his anger and using these techniques, he was able to improve his relationship with his children and become a more confident and effective parent. It wasn't always easy, but he found that with practice and patience, he was able to make significant progress.

I share this story because I want parents to know that they are not alone in their struggles with anger. It's important to remember that we all make mistakes and that it's okay to seek help when we need it. With the right techniques and a commitment to self-improvement, we can all become the best parents we can be.

Let the Work Begin: Distract Yourself With Hobbies

When you feel your anger starting to boil, it's important to have strategies to de-escalate the situation. One way to do this is by distracting yourself with a fun hobby or activity. Use the following list of ideas to create your own personalized list of things you enjoy doing. Circle or check off the ones that sound appealing to you, and keep your list in a place where you can easily access it when you need it.

- Reading a book or magazine
- Listening to music or a podcast
- Taking a walk or bike ride
- Painting or drawing
- Cooking or baking
- Playing a musical instrument
- Doing a puzzle or playing a game
- Writing in a journal or blog

- Dancing or exercising
- Gardening or doing yard work
- Watching a movie or TV show
- Trying a new craft or DIY project
- Taking a relaxing bath or shower
- Meditating or practicing yoga
- Spending time with a pet
- Talking to a friend or family member
- Doing something spontaneous or adventurous
- Going on a nature hike or exploring a new place
- Trying a new restaurant or recipe
- Learning a new skill or language

Remember, the key to using hobbies to stop anger in its tracks is to choose activities that you genuinely enjoy and that can take your mind off the situation. By creating your own personalized list, you'll be better prepared to distract yourself and calm down in moments of stress or frustration.

In this chapter, we have discussed how to prevent ourselves from reacting in anger during moments of heightened stress or frustration. The chapter covers various techniques such as taking a pause, identifying triggers, and communicating effectively. The interactive element of this chapter is about distracting oneself with hobbies when feeling angry.

The key takeaway from this chapter is that anger is a natural emotion, but it's important to learn how to manage it effectively to prevent it from damaging our relationships and mental health. By taking a moment to pause and identify our triggers, we can learn to respond to situations in a more calm and rational manner. Effective communication can also assist in defusing tension and resolving disputes.

In the next chapter, we will discuss using mindfulness to combat anger.

Chapter 9:

Breathe In, Breathe Out—The Power of Mindfulness

Mindfulness... Is this another "new age" word that isn't really going to help me?

In a world that moves quickly, it's simple to get caught up in the commotion of daily life. Many parents tend to feel overwhelmed like they are constantly treading water to keep up with everything. In such moments, it's crucial to take a step back and focus on the present moment.

In this chapter, we will explore the power of mindfulness and how it can help you as a parent. From simple breathing exercises to guided meditations, we will provide you with the tools you need to incorporate mindfulness into your daily routine.

Why Mindfulness is More than a "New Age" Buzzword

Mindfulness is a term that is often thrown around in popular culture, but what does it actually mean? Being totally present and involved in the present moment is the essence of mindfulness. It entails conscious and judgment-free concentration on your thoughts, feelings, and physical experiences. This practice can be applied to any situation, whether it be doing household chores, having a conversation with a loved one, or simply sitting quietly and observing your surroundings.

Meditation is often associated with mindfulness, and for a good reason. Meditation is a specific technique used to cultivate mindfulness. During meditation, you sit quietly and focus your attention on your breath or a specific point of focus. This helps you to become more aware of your thoughts and feelings, and over time, it can help you to develop a greater sense of calm and clarity.

There are several types of meditation, including mantra, body scan, and movement meditation. For some individuals, practicing mindfulness while completing daily tasks, like washing dishes or taking a walk, can be useful. These meditation methods are just as effective for developing awareness as sitting meditation.

The seven pillars of mindfulness, as outlined by Jon Kabat-Zinn, provide a helpful framework for understanding the various components of mindfulness practice. These tenets include non-judgment, patience, trust, beginner's mentality, non-striving, acceptance, and letting go. For the development of mindfulness in daily life, each of these pillars is crucial. For example, non-judging involves observing your thoughts and feelings without attaching a value judgment to them. This can help you to become more aware of your automatic thought patterns and develop a greater sense of self-awareness.

The breath awareness meditation is a straightforward meditation technique that might assist you in developing mindfulness. Choose a peaceful area where you won't be bothered to practice this method. With your eyes closed and your back straight, take a comfortable seat. After a few deep breaths to ground yourself, start concentrating on your breathing. Take note of how your breath feels as it enters and leaves your body. Bring your focus back on the breath whenever it begins to stray. Spend five to ten minutes practicing this, or more if you'd like.

Overall, mindfulness is more than just a "new age" buzzword. It is a powerful practice that can help you to cultivate greater self-awareness, reduce stress and anxiety, and improve your overall well-being. By incorporating mindfulness into your daily routine, you can learn to be more present and engaged in your life and develop a greater sense of inner peace and calm.

Mindful Parenting

Parenting with mindfulness is the application of awareness to the experience. It means bringing conscious awareness to the present moment while engaging with your children. Mindful parenting is about responding to your child's needs instead of reacting impulsively to their behavior. This means that instead of being on autopilot, you are intentionally focusing on the present moment without judgment.

In contrast to mindfulness, which is a broader practice of being present in all areas of life, mindful parenting is about using mindfulness techniques to enhance the parent-child relationship. It means approaching parenting from a place of compassion, empathy, and patience rather than frustration and impatience. Mindful parenting involves paying attention to your child's cues, listening actively, and responding with openness and non-judgment.

Among the main advantages of mindful parenting is that it may improve how well you control your emotions. By bringing mindful awareness to the present moment, you can recognize when your emotions are becoming overwhelming and choose to respond in a way that is more measured and controlled. Mindful parenting can also help you develop a deeper connection with your child, as it enables you to give your child your full attention and engage with them in a more present and authentic way.

Mindful parenting is a practice that involves bringing your conscious attention to your parenting experiences, being present in the moment with your child, and responding to them with compassion and understanding. By practicing mindful parenting, you can become more aware of your own emotions and reactions, as well as those of your child, and be better equipped to respond rather than react in difficult situations.

One of the biggest benefits of mindful parenting is that it can help you develop a stronger relationship with your child. When you are fully present with your child, you are able to truly listen and connect with them on a deeper level. You are also more likely to respond to their needs in a compassionate and understanding way, which can help them feel safe, secure, and loved.

You may effectively practice mindful parenting by adhering to a few essential components. These include:

- **Being present**: Being fully present with your child is the first step to practicing mindful parenting. It means letting go of distractions and focusing all of your attention on your child and the present moment.
- **Non-judgment**: Non-judgment means accepting your child and their experiences without judgment or criticism. It involves letting go of your own

preconceived notions and biases and seeing things from your child's perspective.

- **Compassion**: Compassion involves responding to your child with kindness, understanding, and empathy. It means acknowledging their emotions and needs and responding to them in a way that is caring and supportive.

- **Self-regulation**: Self-regulation involves being aware of your own emotions and reactions and learning to manage them in a healthy and constructive way. By practicing self-regulation, you can avoid reacting impulsively or angrily to your child's behavior and respond in a more thoughtful and intentional way.

There are several ways to practice mindful parenting, including breathing exercises, guided meditation, and mindfulness activities. Breathing exercises can help you stay calm and centered in stressful situations, while guided meditation can help you develop greater awareness and focus. Mindfulness activities, such as mindful eating or mindful walks, can also help you develop a greater presence and connection with your child.

In conclusion, mindful parenting may make you a more aware, sympathetic, and successful parent. By focusing on the present moment and responding to your child's needs with kindness and understanding, you can develop a stronger relationship with your child and create a more positive and fulfilling parenting experience.

Breathing Your Way to Calm

Deep, slow breathing exercises may be helpful for you in many ways, including lowering blood pressure, enhancing sleep, decreasing discomfort, and enhancing focus. When you're feeling overwhelmed, taking a few deep breaths can help calm your mind and body, bringing you back to a more centered state. This can be especially useful in stressful situations, where taking a moment to breathe deeply can help you to respond in a more mindful and effective way.

Studies have shown that deep breathing can help to reduce anxiety by activating the body's relaxation response, which can help to lower blood pressure and slow down your heart rate (Ma et al., 2017). Easing the physical signs of tension and worry that might make it difficult to fall asleep or remain asleep, may also help you achieve better-quality sleep. Deep breathing can also help to reduce pain by increasing the flow of oxygen to the body, which can help to relax muscles and reduce tension.

Improved focus is an advantage of deep breathing as well. When you're feeling stressed or anxious, it can be difficult to focus on the task at hand. By taking a few deep breaths and bringing your attention to your breath, you can clear your mind and improve your ability to concentrate.

Breathing exercises aren't just beneficial for adults; they can also be helpful for children and teens. Teaching your children to practice deep breathing exercises is an excellent way to help them learn how to calm down and manage their emotions when they are feeling overwhelmed. Here are some benefits of breathing exercises for kids and some tips on how to go through these exercises with them:

Benefits of Breathing Exercises for Children and Teens

- **Boosts relaxation**: Breathing exercises can make kids and teenagers feel less stressed and more calm.

- **Improved concentration**: These exercises help to increase focus and concentration in children, which can be particularly useful for those who struggle with attention issues.

- **Quality rest**: One way to improve the quality of sleep for your children is through deep breathing exercises, which may help them fall asleep more quickly and stay asleep throughout the night.

- **Less pain**: Breathing exercises can help children and teens manage physical pain, such as headaches or stomach aches, by promoting relaxation.

Tips for Going Through Breathing Exercises with Children and Teens

- **Start with simple exercises**: Start by guiding your child on basic breathing techniques, such as deep inhalations and exhalations via the nose and mouth.

- **Make it fun**: Incorporate fun games or stories into your breathing exercises. For example, you can ask your child to imagine they are blowing up a balloon with their breath or have them pretend they are blowing out birthday candles.

- **Be patient**: It may take some time for your child to feel comfortable with deep breathing exercises, so be patient and keep practicing.

- **Encourage regular practice**: To get the most benefit from breathing exercises, it's important to practice them regularly. Schedule daily time to perform these activities with your kid.

- **Set a good example**: Children frequently imitate their parents, so by engaging in deep breathing exercises, you may influence your child to do the same.

Overall, deep breathing exercises are an excellent way to help your child or teen learn how to calm down and manage their emotions when they are feeling overwhelmed. By incorporating these exercises into your daily routine, you can help your child develop important skills that will serve them well throughout their lives.

Breathing Exercises

For lengthening your exhale, start by inhaling for a count of four, then exhaling for a count of six or eight. You can gradually increase the length of your exhale over time as you get comfortable with the exercise.

For breath focus, simply bring your attention to the sensation of your breath moving in and out of your body. You can do this for a few minutes at a time throughout the day or use it as a quick way to refocus your attention during moments of stress.

Equal breathing is a breathing exercise that involves inhaling and exhaling for an equal amount of time. This technique typically involves inhaling and exhaling for a count of four, but the length of the breath can be adjusted to suit individual needs. Practicing equal breathing is believed to promote balance and calmness in both the body and mind.

In order to breathe in a way known as resonance, one must inhale for four counts, hold their breath for seven counts, and then exhale for eight counts. This exercise has been shown to help reduce stress and anxiety and can be especially helpful for people who tend to over-breathe or hyperventilate.

Lion's breath is a more dynamic exercise that involves taking a deep inhale through the nose, then exhaling loudly while sticking out your tongue and making a "ha" sound. This exercise can help release tension and promote relaxation.

Finally, alternate nostril breathing involves using your fingers to alternate which nostril you are breathing through. Start by inhaling through one nostril for a count of four, then exhaling through the other nostril for a count of four. Repeat on the other side. This exercise can help balance the flow of energy in the body and promote a sense of calm and relaxation.

The Power of Meditation

As a parent, you are no stranger to the feelings of anger that can arise from time to time. Whether it is the stress of work, financial worries, or just the daily chaos of parenting, it is easy to get overwhelmed and lose your temper. However, meditation has been proven to be an effective tool for combating anger and achieving a sense of calm and peace in your life.

Meditation has been shown to be an effective tool for managing anger because it helps to regulate the negative emotions that can lead to anger outbursts. Meditation works by training your mind to focus on the present moment, which can help you to let go of negative thoughts and emotions. By doing this, you can learn to control your reactions to triggers that might otherwise cause you to become angry.

But the benefits of meditation go beyond just anger management. Meditation may help you become a more patient and compassionate parent, improve your overall mood and well-being, and even improve your physical health. Studies have demonstrated that meditation helps lower blood pressure, lessen tension and anxiety, and enhance sleep.

How, then, do you begin practicing meditation? The first step is to find a quiet, comfortable place where you can sit or lie down without distractions. Set a timer for the length of time you want to meditate and focus on your breath. Pay attention to the sensation of the air entering and leaving your body, and if your mind wanders, gently bring it back to your breath. It is important to remember that meditation is not about achieving a certain state of mind but rather about observing your thoughts and feelings without judgment.

It is also important to note that there are many different types of meditation, and you may need to experiment to find the one that works best for you. Some people find that guided meditations, which are led by a teacher or recorded voice, are helpful. Others prefer to meditate in silence or with the help of a mantra or visualization.

If you are new to meditation, it is a good idea to start with shorter sessions and gradually increase the length of time you meditate as you become more comfortable. You can also try different types of meditation to see what works best for you.

Overall, meditation is a powerful tool for parents who want to become more patient, compassionate, and in control of their emotions. By taking the time to meditate each day, you can learn to manage your anger and other negative emotions and become a happier, more present parent.

Story

While working with various parents who struggle to manage their anger, I have had an encounter with one dad who was resistant to trying any breathing exercises or meditation. He kept insisting that they were too "hippie-dippie" for his taste. Despite my attempts to persuade him to give them a chance, he simply wasn't interested.

However, his wife was more receptive and eager to try anything that would help them both. She began practicing breathing exercises and meditation on her own and even encouraged her husband to join her. Finally, after much persuasion, he agreed to give it a try with her.

To his surprise, he felt instantly calmer after just a few minutes of mindful breathing. With continued practice, he was able to maintain his calm and control his anger better in everyday situations.

Another mom I worked with was struggling to maintain her composure with her children. She often found herself becoming impatient and reactive when her kids were misbehaving or not listening to her. She began incorporating daily meditation into her routine and noticed a significant improvement in her patience and ability to stay calm in difficult situations.

These stories serve as a reminder of the power of mindfulness and meditation in helping parents manage their anger and stay present with their children. While it may take some time and effort to get started, the benefits are well worth it. So, if you're struggling with anger as a parent, consider giving mindfulness and meditation a chance. You might be surprised at how much it can help you.

Let the work begin: Belly Breathing to Tame the Beast Inside

If you are tired of feeling like a ticking time bomb ready to explode with anger at any moment, try Belly Breathing! With just a few minutes of practice, you can learn to control your breathing and find calm amidst the chaos of parenting. Hence, let's begin your quest for a happy, healthier self.

1. Step 1: Find a comfortable and quiet place to sit down.
2. Step 2: Place your hands on your stomach, right below your rib cage.
3. Step 3: Inhale through your nose slowly, allowing your stomach to expand like a balloon. You should feel your hands move outwards as you inhale.
4. Step 4: Briefly hold your breath.
5. Step 5: Exhale slowly through your mouth, allowing your stomach to collapse. You should feel your hands move inward as you exhale.
6. Step 6: Repeat this cycle for 2-3 minutes or until you feel your body and mind start to relax.

This exercise can be done anytime and anywhere and is especially helpful when you feel your anger starting to rise. Taking a few minutes to focus on your breath and practicing belly breathing can help you calm down and regain control before reacting in anger toward your children.

Guided Meditation for Mom and Dad

When you want to take a break from the chaos of everyday life, give yourself some much-needed relaxation and rejuvenation. We know how hectic and stressful parenting can be, so we've put together a special guided meditation just for you. This meditation will help you to unwind, clear your mind, and find peace within. So, take a deep breath, sit back, and let's begin this journey together!

Before starting a breathing exercise, it's important to find a serene and cozy spot where you won't be disturbed. You can either sit or lie down in a position that feels comfortable to you. After that, close your eyes and take a few deep breaths by inhaling through your nose and exhaling through your mouth. This initial step can assist you in relaxing and getting ready for the breathing exercise.

While continuing with your deep breathing, focus your attention on the physical sensations in your body. Notice any areas of tension or discomfort and allow them to soften with each breath.

Imagine a calm environment where you are entirely at ease and at rest with yourself. It could be a beach, a forest, or any other place that brings you a sense of calm. Visualize this place in your mind's eye and allow yourself to feel fully immersed in its peaceful energy.

As you stay in this peaceful place, focus on your breath. Notice the sensation of the air moving in and out of your body. Imagine that with each inhale, you're breathing in a sense of calm and relaxation. And with each exhale, you're releasing any tension or stress.

Now, bring your attention to your thoughts. You might notice that your mind is busy with worries or to-do lists. This is completely normal. Simply observe your thoughts without judgment and let them pass like clouds in the sky.

As you continue to focus on your breath, imagine that you're breathing in love and compassion for yourself. Imagine that you're sending yourself kind and supportive thoughts. Repeat to yourself silently, "I am doing my best" or "I am a loving and patient parent."

Take a few more deep breaths, and when you're ready, slowly open your eyes. Observe your feelings for a moment. Remember that you can return to this peaceful place and this sense of calm whenever you need it.

In this chapter, we discussed how mindfulness can help you become more aware of your thoughts and feelings while allowing you to respond to situations in calm and constructive ways. The interactive element included a belly breathing exercise and guided meditation to help you practice mindfulness.

Key takeaways from this chapter include the importance of self-awareness and taking a pause to breathe and collect oneself before responding to a stressful situation. It is also important to acknowledge and accept one's emotions without judgment and to practice self-compassion and forgiveness.

The next chapter focuses on repairing relationships with children after experiencing anger and conflict. It will explore how to communicate effectively, apologize when necessary, and work toward healing and strengthening the parent-child bond.

Chapter 10:

Moving Forward—Healing With Your Children

We all make mistakes as parents. We become irrational, say things we don't mean, and act in regrettable ways. And when we do, we frequently feel remorseful, humiliated, and estranged from our kids. But here's the thing: we cannot go back in time. We can't erase the hurtful things we've said or done. What we can do is move forward. We can acknowledge our mistakes, take responsibility for our actions, and work toward healing with our children. But how do we do that? How do we repair the damage that's been done and rebuild the trust and connection that's been lost? That's what this chapter is all about. We'll explore the steps you can take to move forward with your children, including apologizing, making amends, and rebuilding trust. So, if you're prepared to initiate the healing process for your child, let's begin right away.

It Begins With "I'm Sorry"

As parents, we often think that we need to have all the answers, be perfect, and never make mistakes. However, this is simply not realistic. We all make mistakes, and it's important for us to acknowledge them and apologize when we hurt someone. This is especially true for our children.

One reason why it is important to apologize to your children is that you are their biggest role model. Children are constantly learning from their parents, whether it's how to tie their shoes, how to treat others with kindness, or how to apologize when they make a mistake. By modeling apology and accountability, you are teaching your children an important life skill that they can use in their own relationships.

Children need to understand that you aren't perfect and that they don't have to be either, which is another reason why it's necessary to apologize to them. As parents, we want to be strong and reliable for our children, but we also want them to know that they can make mistakes and still be loved. Apologizing can help to build a relationship of trust with your children, and it can also help them to feel more comfortable admitting their own mistakes.

Apologizing is also essential to growing and having healthy relationships. When we apologize, we acknowledge that we have hurt someone, and we take responsibility for our actions. This can help to repair any damage that has been done to the relationship and can help to build trust and intimacy.

Finally, if you don't apologize, it sends your children the wrong message and teaches them the wrong lessons. If you never apologize, your children may believe that it's okay to hurt others without consequence. On the other hand, if you apologize too much or make excuses for your behavior, your children may learn that it's not okay to make mistakes or take responsibility for their actions. By apologizing when it's appropriate, you can help your children to understand that mistakes happen, but it's important to take responsibility and make things right.

Transition Into Dos and Don'ts of Apologizing to Children

Every parent has their way of expressing their apologies, but not all those approaches are correct. Here is the line between dos and don'ts.

Dos

Apologize easily and often: Apologizing to your child is an essential part of parenting. It can strengthen the parent-child relationship, promote open communication, and set a positive example for your child to follow. One important thing to keep in mind is to apologize easily and often. This means not waiting for your child to bring up a past issue or for an argument to occur. Instead, take the initiative to apologize whenever you feel you have done something wrong, no matter how small the issue may seem.

Acknowledge your child's feelings: Another important part of apologizing is to acknowledge your child's emotions. Although it can be simple to ignore or belittle your child's feelings, doing so can cause them to feel unheard and unimportant. Spend some time acknowledging your child's feelings and perspective when you apologize. Building trust and understanding with your child via this is possible.

Take responsibility for your own feelings: Taking responsibility for your own feelings is also an important aspect of apologizing. It can be tempting to blame others or external factors for our mistakes, but this can prevent us from truly learning and growing from our experiences. Instead, take ownership of your feelings and actions, and show your child that you are committed to making things right.

Describe what happened: Explaining what happened is another helpful step when apologizing to your child. This can help your child understand what went wrong and why you are apologizing. It can also provide an opportunity for you to clarify any misunderstandings and ensure that both you and your child are on the same page.

Talk about ways to prevent a situation like that in the future: Talking about how to avoid a similar situation in the future is another important aspect of apologizing. This can help prevent the same issue from happening again in the future and can show your child that you are committed to making positive changes in your behavior.

Ask if they are ready to forgive: Finally, it is important to ask if your child is ready to forgive. It can be tempting to rush through the apology process and move on, but doing so can prevent your child from fully processing their emotions and can lead to unresolved issues. Instead, take the time to ask if your child is ready to move forward and respect their answer. This can help to build trust and understanding between you and your child and create a more positive, healthy relationship.

Don'ts

Apologizing to a child can be a difficult task, but it is essential to do so in a way that is helpful and effective. But there are some traps to watch out for while saying sorry to a child. Here are some things that you should not do when apologizing to your child:

- **Guilt-Trip**: One of the most important things to avoid when apologizing to your child is making them feel guilty. Guilt-tripping can backfire and make your child feel worse than before. Instead, focus on your behavior and how you can make it better.

- Saying "I'm sorry you feel that way" is not considered a genuine apology, and it may give your child the impression that their emotions are not being respected. Rather than dismissing their feelings, it is essential to acknowledge the impact of your actions and take responsibility for them.

- **Pass Judgment or Blame:** When apologizing to your child, avoid passing judgment or blame on them or others, as it can trigger a defensive response from your child and potentially escalate the situation. Focus on your behavior and how you can improve it.

- **Make Excuses**: Making excuses when apologizing can undermine your apology and make it seem insincere. Instead, take responsibility for your actions and try to make amends.

- **Ignore Why the Problem Happened**: Ignoring why the problem happened in the first place can make it more likely to happen again in the future. Instead, have a discussion with your child about why the situation occurred and how to prevent it from happening again.

Expect Something in Return: When apologizing to your child, it is important to avoid expecting anything in return. This could put too much pressure on your child and make them feel uneasy or apprehensive. Instead, focus on taking responsibility for your actions and making things right.

Moving Forward... Together

The relationship between a parent and child is one of the most important relationships a person can have in their lifetime. It is important to recognize when there are issues within the relationship and to work to fix them in order to create a strong and healthy bond. Failure to do so may have negative consequences for both the parent and the child, as well as for their future relationships.

If issues within the parent-child relationship are not addressed and fixed, it may lead to long-term estrangement or other negative outcomes, such as poor mental health, lack of trust, and emotional distance. As children grow older and become adults, they may choose to distance themselves from their parents due to unresolved conflicts or a lack of emotional connection.

However, there are ways to repair and rebuild a strong and loving relationship with your child. Below are some useful tips that you may find helpful:

- **Say "I love you" often**: These three simple words can go a long way in strengthening your relationship with your child. Saying "I love you" to your child regularly can help them feel secure, loved, and valued.

- **Set aside one-on-one time**: Creating special one-on-one time with your child can help them feel seen and heard. It can be anything from going on a walk together, playing a game, or just having a conversation. The key is to focus on the relationship without distractions.

- **Engage in activities with your child**: Spending time playing and participating in activities with your child can be both enjoyable and beneficial for building a strong relationship. Whether it's playing catch, board games, or video games, engaging in activities together can foster bonding and create positive experiences and memories for you and your child.

- **Eat together**: Eating meals together can be a great way to connect with your child. It provides an opportunity for conversation and bonding over shared experiences.

- **Really listen to them**: One of the most important things you can do for your child is to truly listen to them. Be attentive to your child's thoughts, emotions, and concerns. Avoid interrupting or dismissing them. Let them know that their feelings are valid and that you care.

Story

Once upon a time, I had the pleasure of working with a mother named Adaku, who was struggling with controlling her anger toward her children. Adaku is a proud Nigerian woman who believed that harsh discipline was necessary to raise well-behaved children. It was ingrained in her culture that parents should never apologize to their children, as it was seen as a sign of weakness.

Adaku often found herself shouting at her children, scolding them for the smallest mistakes. While she knew it was not the right thing to do, she found it difficult to break away from her traditional beliefs. She believed that her children's behavior warranted her reaction, and she refused to see it any other way.

It was during one of our sessions that Adaku's perspective began to shift. I asked her to have an open conversation with her son and listen to how he felt when she yelled at him. To her surprise, he said that he felt sad and scared. Then I asked how he would feel if his mother apologized to him, and he said he would be happy.

Adaku was shocked by her son's reply. She had never considered apologizing to her children before, but seeing the effect it could have on them made her think twice. She was torn between her traditional values and the newfound realization that her actions were hurting her children.

As our sessions progressed, I continued to emphasize the importance of apologizing to her children and how it could improve their relationship. Adaku struggled with the idea at first, but eventually, she realized that she needed to put her children's emotional well-being first. She mustered the courage to apologize to her children and promised to work on controlling her temper.

It was not an easy road for Adaku, but with practice, she learned to control her anger and use more positive discipline methods. She found that her relationship with her children grew stronger when she apologized for her mistakes and listened to them when they had something to say. Adaku learned that sometimes, it's okay to break away from tradition and put her children's happiness first.

In the end, Adaku's story is a testament to the power of empathy and open-mindedness. It takes courage to challenge traditional beliefs, but sometimes, it's necessary to create a better future for our children. Adaku's journey may have been difficult, but it allowed her to grow as a person and become a better mother.

Let The Work Begin: Sorry

Apologizing is an essential aspect of healthy relationships. It helps to mend the bond and rebuild trust. The following exercise uses the SORRY acronym to help you offer effective apologies.

1. **Step 1: S—State the action you regret**

    The first step to apologizing is acknowledging what you did wrong. It would be best if you stated what you regret doing, which shows that you're taking responsibility for your actions.

    Example: "I apologize for raising my voice at you earlier."

2. **Step 2: O—Offer an apology**

    Offering an apology is crucial in acknowledging that what you did was wrong and that you're sorry for it.

3. **Step 3: R—Repair the damage**

    After apologizing, you should make an effort to repair the damage caused by your actions. It could be by doing something nice for the person you hurt or finding a way to prevent it from happening again.

    Example: "Let's talk about what I did and figure out how to avoid yelling in the future."

4. **Step 4: R—Responsibility**

   Assume accountability for your actions and recognize the effect they had on your child. It shows that you understand the effect of your actions and are willing to work to fix them.

   Example: "I understand that yelling can be scary, and I'm sorry that I made you feel that way."

5. **Step 5: Y—Yield control**

   The final step is to allow the other person to have control over how to respond. Once you have apologized, it's up to the other person to decide how they want to proceed. Respect their decision and be open to discussing any further concerns or steps that can be taken to make amends.

   Example: "I'm sorry again. What can I do to make things right between us?"

By following the SORRY acronym, readers (parents) can teach their children to apologize effectively as well. Teaching children to take responsibility for their actions, acknowledging the impact of their actions, and repairing the damage caused can help build stronger relationships and foster empathy.

Worksheet

Using the SORRY acronym, write an apology to someone you've hurt in the past. Be sure to follow each step and make it as genuine as possible.

Step 1: S—State the action you regret

Step 2: O—Offer an apology

Step 3: R—Repair the damage

Step 4: R—Responsibility

Step 5: Y—Yield control

Now, think about a situation where your child hurts someone else. Using the SORRY acronym, guide them through the process of apologizing and making amends. Encourage them to take responsibility for their actions and make an effort to repair the damage they caused.

You have walked this path to the end; congratulations.

Conclusion

I hope this book has been helpful in providing insight into understanding and managing anger as a parent. From understanding what triggers your anger to using mindfulness to combat it, we explored various strategies and techniques to help you better control your emotions and build positive relationships with your children.

The main lesson to be learned from this book is that while anger is a normal human emotion if it is not controlled, it can be destructive. It is essential to take responsibility for our emotions, communicate effectively with our children, and prioritize self-care to avoid burnout and improve our well-being.

Here is where you branch onto a new path: the action.

Remember, this is not a one-size-fits-all solution. It takes time and practice to implement these techniques successfully. However, the success stories of other parents who have followed these methods show that with consistent effort, it is possible to make positive changes in your parenting style.

I encourage you to continue practicing the exercises and techniques outlined in this guide, even after you finish reading it. Keep in mind that parenting is a journey full of ups and downs, and setbacks are part of the process. Don't hesitate to take a step back and repeat some exercises if you need to—that is what they are here for.

Taking the time to invest in your growth as a parent was a major step toward positive change. If you found this a helpful read, please consider leaving a review to help other parents benefit from its information as well. In the end, there's hope for our children and us!

To leave a review, all you need to do is revisit the page that has the QR code, then follow the instructions.

References

Abramson, A. (2021a, February 25). *6 phrases that you need to drop to improve your self esteem.* Fatherly. https://www.fatherly.com/love-money/negative-self-talk-phrases-to-avoid

Abramson, A. (2021b, October 1). *The impact of parental burnout.* https://www.apa.org/monitor/2021/10/cover-parental-burnout

American Psychological Association. (2022, March 3). *Controlling anger — before it controls you.* https://www.apa.org. https://www.apa.org/topics/anger/control

American Psychological Association. (n.d.). *Anger and aggression.* https://www.apa.org. https://www.apa.org/topics/anger

Ankrom, S. (2021, March 20). *How to breathe properly for relieving your anxiety.* Verywell Mind. https://www.verywellmind.com/abdominal-breathing-2584115

Arens, N. (2021, January 28). *The importance of mom friends.* https://www.coliccalm.com/blog/post/the-importance-of-mom-friends

Austin, D. (2022, December 28). *6 reasons why yelling at kids doesn't actually work.* Parents.

https://www.parents.com/health/healthy-happy-kids/a-parental-wake-up-call-yelling-doesnt-help/

Australia, H. (2020, November 23). *Controlling your anger as a parent.* https://www.pregnancybirthbaby.org.au/controlling-your-anger-as-a-parent

Bandura, A. (2008). *Observational learning.* The International Encyclopedia of Communication. https://doi.org/10.1002/9781405186407.wbieco004

Banks, C. (n.d.). *Disrespectful child behavior? Don't take it personally.* Empowering Parents. https://www.empoweringparents.com/article/disrespectful-child-behavior-dont-take-it-personally/

Bennett, T. (2019, January 22). *Are some people genetically prone to anger? Can anger run in families?.* https://thriveworks.com/blog/are-some-people-genetically-prone-to-anger-can-anger-run-in-families/

Better sleep. (2022, September 15). *How to use meditation for anger control.* www.bettersleep.com. https://www.bettersleep.com/blog/how-to-use-meditation-for-anger-control/

Bickle, L. (2020, March 7). *How to discipline a toddler? 12 tactics that actually work.* Today's Parent. https://www.todaysparent.com/family/discipline/toddler-discipline/

Bonior Ph.D., A. (2022, September 29). *6 things not to do during an apology.* www.psychologytoday.com.

144

https://www.psychologytoday.com/us/blog/friendship-20/202209/6-things-not-do-during-apology

Brain Training Australia.com. (n.d.). *Assertive anger.* https://www.braintrainingaustralia.com/anger/assertive-anger/

Brennan, D. (2021). *What to know about 4-7-8 breathing.* https://www.webmd.com/balance/what-to-know-4-7-8-breathing

Bryan, K. (2017, February 20). *5 reasons why adult children estrange from their parents.* https://wehavekids.com/family-relationships/adult-child-estranged-reasons

Campaigns, T. M. (2022, November 7). *Reduce tension and stress with belly breathing.* The Monday Campaigns. https://www.mondaycampaigns.org/destress-monday/belly-breathing

CDC. (2019). *Active listening.* https://www.cdc.gov/parents/essentials/communication/activelistening.html

Ceder, J. (2019). *How inconsistent parenting can cause behavior problems.* Verywell Family. https://www.verywellfamily.com/why-does-consistency-matter-in-parenting-4135227

Ceder, J. (2023, January 30). *Mindful parenting: How to respond instead of react.* The Gottman Institute. https://www.gottman.com/blog/mindful-parenting-how-to-respond-instead-of-react/

Cody, T. (2022, January 28). *Wondering how to heal your emotional triggers? These 8 strategies will help.* https://www.ipeccoaching.com/blog/how-to-heal-emotional-triggers

Cuncic, A. (2022, November 9). *How to practice active listening.* Verywell Mind. https://www.verywellmind.com/what-is-active-listening-3024343

D. Flaxington, B. (2020, February 4). *The destructive nature of negative self-talk.* www.psychologytoday.com. https://www.psychologytoday.com/us/blog/understand-other-people/202002/the-destructive-nature-negative-self-talk

Daniel, S. (2015, March 25). *When mom needs a timeout - taking a break from your children.* www.professorshouse.com. https://www.professorshouse.com/when-mom-needs-a-timeout/

Dhole, J. (2022, March 16). *How to identify parenting triggers and 10 ways to deal with them.* Times of India Blog. https://timesofindia.indiatimes.com/readersblog/parenting-journey/how-to-identify-parenting-triggers-and-10-ways-to-deal-with-them-41867/

Doucleff, M., & Greenhalgh, J. (2019, March 13). *NPR choice page.* https://www.npr.org/sections/goatsandsoda/2019/03/13/685533353/a-playful-way-to-teach-kids-to-control-their-anger

DPS Staff. (2021, April 23). *10 ways to practice positive self-talk.* https://www.delawarepsychologicalservices.com/post/10-ways-to-practice-positive-self-talk

Dye, H. (2018). The impact and long-term effects of childhood trauma. *Journal of Human Behavior in the Social Environment, 28*(3), 381–392. https://doi.org/10.1080/10911359.2018.1435328

Early Development (2021, September 6). *What is positive discipline and why is it important?.* https://www.earlydevelopment.org/what-is-positive-discipline/

EHN Canada. (2021, October 6). *The seven pillars of mindfulness.* https://www.edgewoodhealthnetwork.com/resources/blog/the-seven-pillars-of-mindfulness/

Estévez, E., Góngora, J., Universidad, & Altamira, E. (n.d.). *Adolescent aggression towards parents: Factors associated and intervention proposals.* https://www.uv.es/lisis/estevez/handbook-agresive-behav.pdf

Family Education. (2006, July 5). *Tips on listening to your child.* FamilyEducation. https://www.familyeducation.com/life/communicating-your-child/tips-listening-your-child

Finds, S. (2021, March 22). *Frequently yelling at your children may wind up shrinking their brains, scientist warns.* https://studyfinds.org/yelling-at-children-harsh-parenting-shrinking-brains/

Gabbey, A. E. (2013). *Aggressive behavior.* https://www.healthline.com/health/aggressive-behavior

Gamble, L. (2019, October 20). *Stop being so hard on yourself: 5 reasons why you're a great parent.* Babyology. https://babyology.com.au/toddler/learning-and-development/stop-being-so-hard-on-yourself-5-reasons-why-youre-a-great-parent/

Glicksman, E. (2019, May). *Physical discipline is harmful and ineffective.* https://www.apa.org/monitor/2019/05/physical-discipline

Glowiak, M. (2020, April 14). *What is self-care and why is it important for you?* www.snhu.edu. https://www.snhu.edu/about-us/newsroom/health/what-is-self-care

Goldman, R. (2017, April 19). *5 ways yelling hurts kids in the long run.* Healthline. https://www.healthline.com/health/parenting/effects-of-yelling-at-kids

Gotter, A. (2019, April 22). *8 breathing exercises for anxiety you can try right now.* Healthline. https://www.healthline.com/health/breathing-exercises-for-anxiety#alternate-nostrils

Greene, A. L., Sharon. (n.d.). *Signs that you may have anger issues and how to cope with it.* Insider. https://www.insider.com/anger-issues

Grenny, J. (2016, March 22). *Repairing relationships with your children.* Crucial Learning. https://cruciallearning.com/blog/repairing-relationships-with-your-children/

Gresko, B. (2015, June 22). *No guilt allowed! Why parents need time for themselves.* https://quietrev.com/why-parents-need-alone-time/

Harrison, P. (2018, May 2). *21 examples of negative self talk & negative thoughts that kill.* The Daily Meditation Coaching Sessions. https://www.thedailymeditation.com/7-types-of-negative-thinking-you-seriously-need-to-kill

Harvey, B. (2015, December 21). *Positive parenting defined.* Kars4Kids Parenting. https://parenting.kars4kids.org/positive-parenting-defined/

Hax, B. C. (2010, February 22). *Spilled water anger: Symptom of being bad father?* https://www.seattlepi.com/lifestyle/advice/article/Spilled-water-anger-Symptom-of-being-bad-father-896180.php

Health Coach Institute. (2021, September 6). *7 types of self-care & why you need them.* https://www.healthcoachinstitute.com/articles/7-types-of-self-care/

Hilary. (2017, August 14). *How to stay calm when your kids destroy your clean house.* HilaryBernstein.com. https://hilarybernstein.com/when-your-kids-fight-order/

Jacoblund, E. E. |. (2020, January 8). *10 self-care tips for parents.* MGH Clay Center for Young Healthy Minds. https://www.mghclaycenter.org/parenting-concerns/10-self-care-tips-for-parents/

Janelled. (2019). *Self-Care for parents — PEPS.* https://www.peps.org/ParentResources/by-topic/self-care/self-care-for-parents

Kalpana M. (2019, July 30). *Parent-Child relationship: Why is it important and how to build it.* https://www.momjunction.com/articles/helpful-tips-to-strengthen-parent-child-bonding_0079667/

Kenney, J. (2017, March 23). *25 ways I cut myself slack on A difficult mom day.* Romper. https://www.romper.com/p/25-little-ways-i-cut-myself-some-slack-on-my-most-difficult-mom-days-46150

Kentucky Counseling center. (2021, February 8). *8 signs you have ANGER ISSUES and how to OVERCOME it.* https://kentuckycounselingcenter.com/8-signs-you-have-anger-issues-and-overcoming-them/

Kryza, A. (2017, October 24). *So you completely freaked out in front of your kid.* here's what to do next. Fatherly. https://www.fatherly.com/parenting/parents-freak-out-angry-at-kid-after/

Lee, K. (2019). *Keep tone and words positive when communicating with your child.* Verywell Family. https://www.verywellfamily.com/how-do-you-talk-to-your-child-620058

Lerner, C. (n.d.). *Responsive vs. reactive parenting: It makes all the difference.* https://www.pbs.org/parents/thrive/responsive-vs-reactive-parenting-it-makes-all-the-difference

Li, P. (2022, February 23). *Reactive parenting - what it is & how to overcome.* Parenting for Brain. https://www.parentingforbrain.com/reactive-parenting/

Ma, X., Yue, Z.-Q., Gong, Z.-Q., Zhang, H., Duan, N.-Y., Shi, Y.-T., Wei, G.-X., & Li, Y.-F. (2017). The effect of diaphragmatic breathing on attention, negative affect and stress in healthy adults. *Frontiers in Psychology, 8*(874), 1–12. https://doi.org/10.3389/fpsyg.2017.00874

Maclellan, J. (2020, April 9). *Cut yourself some slack, parenting in a pandemic is a rough gig.* New West Record. https://www.newwestrecord.ca/opinion/blog-cut-yourself-some-slack-parenting-in-a-pandemic-is-a-rough-gig-3120770

Manis, E. (2015, June 30). *Why do I freak-out at my kids (and how can I stop)?* https://therapybeyondthecouch.com/why-do-i-over-react-to-my-kids-and-how-do-i-stop/

Mansfield, B. (2021, August 26). *The way we talk to our children becomes their inner voice.* Your Modern Family. https://www.yourmodernfamily.com/way-talk-children-becomes-inner-voice/

Mantracare Author. (2022, May 27). *Assertive anger: Meaning, types, causes, effects and tips.* Mantra Care.

https://maaggressive-bntracare.org/therapy/anger/assertive-anger/

Marcin, A. (2019, August 21). *Mindful parenting: Definition, examples, and benefits.* Healthline. https://www.healthline.com/health/parenting/mindful-parenting#key-factors

Marie, S. (2022, March 25). *All about mindful parenting.* Psych Central. https://psychcentral.com/health/mindful-parenting

Mayo Clinic Staff. (2022, February 3). *Positive thinking: Stop negative self-talk to reduce stress.* Mayo Clinic. https://www.mayoclinic.org/healthy-lifestyle/stress-management/in-depth/positive-thinking/art-20043950

Mayo Clinic. (n.d.). *How to spot passive-aggressive behavior.* Mayo Clinic. https://www.mayoclinic.org/healthy-lifestyle/adult-health/expert-answers/passive-aggressive-behavior/faq-20057901

McCready, A. (2015, April 11). *7 steps for apologizing to your child.* Positive Parenting Solutions. https://www.positiveparentingsolutions.com/parenting/apologizing-to-your-child

McCready, A. (2021, December 4). *Here's what makes "positive parenting" different—and why experts say it's one of the best parenting styles.* CNBC. https://www.cnbc.com/2021/12/04/why-psychologists-say-positive-parenting-is-the-best-style-for-raising-confident-successful-kids.html

McKlveen, J. M., Morano, R. L., Fitzgerald, M., Zoubovsky, S., Cassella, S. N., Scheimann, J. R., Ghosal, S., Mahbod, P., Packard, B. A., Myers, B., Baccei, M. L., & Herman, J. P. (2016). Chronic Stress Increases Prefrontal Inhibition: A Mechanism for Stress-Induced Prefrontal Dysfunction. *Biological Psychiatry, 80*(10), 754–764. https://doi.org/10.1016/j.biopsych.2016.03.2101

Mental health center. (2019, April 3). *How childhood trauma affects us as adults.* Mental Health Center. https://www.mentalhealthcenter.org/how-childhood-trauma-affects-adult-relationships/

Mindful. (2018). *Getting started with mindfulness.* Mindful. https://www.mindful.org/meditation/mindfulness-getting-started/

Mindful. (2019, April 13). *How to meditate.* Mindful. https://www.mindful.org/how-to-meditate/

Miraglia, L. (2021, January 31). *How constant yelling affects a child's mental health.* Moms. https://www.moms.com/how-constant-yelling-affects-child-mental-health/

Monahan, J. B. (2018, August 20). *How to reclaim the joy, curiosity and carefreeness of childhood.* Medium. https://medium.com/@jennifermonahan_28426/how-to-reclaim-the-joy-curiosity-and-carefreeness-of-childhood-6d10acfa1ca

Moriarty, D. (2022, December 1). *3 pitfalls to avoid when apologizing to your child.* https://www.familyeducation.com/parenting-style/3-pitfalls-to-avoid-when-apologizing-to-your-child

Morin, A. (2018). *Examples of household rules for the entire family*. Verywell Family. https://www.verywellfamily.com/examples-of-household-rules-for-the-entire-family-1094879

Morin, A. (2019). *Discipline strategies for children who hit their parents*. Verywell Family. https://www.verywellfamily.com/what-should-i-do-when-my-child-hits-me-1095004

Morin, A. (2019b). *How to address kids' behavior problems effectively with consequences*. Verywell Family. https://www.verywellfamily.com/make-consequences-more-effective-1094774

Morin, A. (2019c). *15 self-care strategies for busy parents*. Verywell Family. https://www.verywellfamily.com/self-care-for-parents-4178010

National Institute of Health. (2015, September 4). *NIH-led study identifies genetic variant that can lead to severe impulsivity*. https://www.nih.gov/news-events/news-releases/nih-led-study-identifies-genetic-variant-can-lead-severe-impulsivity

National Institute of Mental Health. (2021). *Caring for your mental health*. https://www.nimh.nih.gov/health/topics/caring-for-your-mental-health

NCCIH. (2022, June). *Meditation and mindfulness: What you need to know*. https://www.nccih.nih.gov/health/meditation-and-mindfulness-what-you-need-to-know#

Nelsen, Dr. J. (2016, January 6). *Positive time out*. www.positivediscipline.com. https://www.positivediscipline.com/articles/positive-time-out

Nichols, H. (2019, August 27). *Why am I so angry? Causes and what to do*. https://www.medicalnewstoday.com/articles/326155

Norman, R. E., Byambaa, M., De, R., Butchart, A., Scott, J., & Vos, T. (2012). The long-term health consequences of child physical abuse, emotional abuse, and neglect: A systematic review and meta-analysis. *PLoS Medicine, 9*(11), e1001349. https://doi.org/10.1371/journal.pmed.1001349

Ohwovoriole, T. (2021, May 28). *How to manage your anger*. Verywell Mind. https://www.verywellmind.com/what-is-anger-5120208

Optimistminds. (2020, July 19). *How does an angry parent affect a child?* https://optimistminds.com/how-does-an-angry-parent-affect-a-child/

Parenting NI. (2018, October 25). *Parent-Child relationship - why it's important - parenting NI*. https://www.parentingni.org/blog/parent-child-relationship-why-its-important/

Park, N., Peterson, C., Szvarca, D., Vander Molen, R. J., Kim, E. S., & Collon, K. (2014). Positive psychology and physical health. *American Journal of Lifestyle Medicine, 10*(3), 200–206. https://doi.org/10.1177/1559827614550277

Pendley, J. S. (2016). *Sibling rivalry (for parents) - kidshealth.* https://kidshealth.org/en/parents/sibling-rivalry.html

Perry, B. D. (2009). Examining child maltreatment through a neurodevelopmental lens: Clinical applications of the neurosequential model of therapeutics. *Journal of Loss and Trauma, 14*(4), 240–255. https://doi.org/10.1080/15325020903004350

Pietro, S. (2016, February 25). *How to handle tantrums and meltdowns.* Child Mind Institute; Child Mind Institute. https://childmind.org/article/how-to-handle-tantrums-and-meltdowns/

Planned Parenthood. (2020). *Six types of self care.* Everyaction.com. https://secure.everyaction.com/p/Pg5bqblugE6-NGId09RIcQ2

Positive Discipline. (2018, November 21). *About positive discipline.* https://www.positivediscipline.com/about-positive-discipline

Psychology Today. (2019). *Anger.* https://www.psychologytoday.com/us/basics/anger

Raising Children Network. (2021, May 31). *Effective communication with parents: For professionals.* https://raisingchildren.net.au/for-professionals/working-with-parents/communicating-with-parents/communication-with-parents

Raypole, C. (2020, July 8). *8 tips for healing your inner child.* Healthline.

https://www.healthline.com/health/mental-health/inner-child-healing

Santos-Longhurst, A. (2019, February 4). *Do I have anger issues? How to identify and treat an angry outlook.* https://www.healthline.com/health/anger-issues

Scharff, C. (2015, May 18). *6 ways to rebuild a relationship with your children.* https://www.huffpost.com/entry/6-ways-to-rebuild-a-relationship-with-your-children_b_7294726

Schilling, E. (2018). *Temper tantrums (for parents).* https://kidshealth.org/en/parents/tantrums.html

Schore, A. N. (2001). *Effects of a secure attachment relationship on right brain development, affect regulation, and infant mental health.* https://psycnet.apa.org/record/2001-16734-001

Seto, C. (2023, February 24). *Mom rage is a real thing—here's how to deal with it.* https://www.todaysparent.com/family/family-health/mom-rage-is-a-real-thing-heres-how-to-deal-with-it/

Shabazz, S. (2018, March 17). *Sometimes you need to walk away from your kid — and that's okay.* Scary Mommy. https://www.scarymommy.com/okay-walk-away-from-child

Sibonney, C. (2021, March 3). *This might be why you're getting so mad at your kids.* Today's Parent. https://www.todaysparent.com/family/parenting/parenting-triggers/

Silvestro, S. (2019, July 1). *The power of apologizing to your kids.* https://www.drstevesilvestro.com/power-of-apologizing-to-your-kids

Sisson, K. (2020, December 23). *I feel guilty for wanting alone time, and I can't be the only one.* The Everymom. https://theeverymom.com/i-feel-guilty-for-wanting-alone-time-as-a-mom/

Sorgen, C. (2006, April 6). *Anger management: Counting to 10 and beyond.* https://www.webmd.com/sex-relationships/features/anger-management-counting-to-ten

Soule, K. (2021, April 14). *What to do when it feels like you're gonna lose it.* https://www.scarymommy.com/parenting/when-it-feels-like-youre-gonna-lose-it

Stepping Forward Counseling. (2019, September 11). *The parent timeout: What to do when your emotions are out of control.* Stepping Forward Counseling Center. https://www.steppingforwardcounselingcenter.com/the-parent-timeout/

Strauss, E. (2018). *Parents, stop feeling so guilty about TV time.* https://www.cnn.com/2018/09/20/health/screentime-guilt-parenting-strauss/index.html

Study (2022). *Aggressive parents.* Study.com. https://study.com/academy/lesson/how-aggressive-parents-affect-children.html#

Thakrar, T. (2020, August 6). *The rage cleanse: 6 cleaning tasks to help you blow off steam.*

https://www.goodhomes.co.in/design-and-style/do-it-yourself/the-rage-cleanse-6-cleaning-tasks-to-help-you-blow-off-steam-6535.html

Thorpe, D. (2013, January 10). *How to break the cycle of anger.* FamilyToday. https://www.familytoday.com/self-care/how-to-break-the-cycle-of-anger/

Todayskids. (2021, October 15). Cut yourself some slack. Today's Kids in Motion Magazine. https://www.todayskids.ca/featured-carousel/cut-yourself-some-slack/

Tomoda, A., Sheu, Y.-S., Rabi, K., Suzuki, H., Navalta, C. P., Polcari, A., & Teicher, M. H. (2011). Exposure to parental verbal abuse is associated with increased gray matter volume in superior temporal gyrus. *NeuroImage, 54* Suppl *1,* S280-6. https://doi.org/10.1016/j.neuroimage.2010.05.027

Wang, M.-T., & Kenny, S. (2013). Longitudinal links between fathers' and mothers' harsh verbal discipline and adolescents' conduct problems and depressive symptoms. *Child Development, 85*(3), 908–923. https://doi.org/10.1111/cdev.12143

Watkins Publishing. (2017, June 26). *Writing a letter to your inner child.* Mental Movement Magazine. https://www.mentalmovement.co.uk/writing-a-letter-to-your-inner-child/

Watkins, E. R. (2008). Constructive and unconstructive repetitive thought. *Psychological Bulletin, 134*(2), 163–206. https://doi.org/10.1037/0033-2909.134.2.163

Wrigh, J., & Tieperman, J. (2021, August 25). *How to talk to children*. https://www.wikihow.com/Talk-to-Children

www.ingramcontent.com/pod-product-compliance
Lightning Source LLC
Chambersburg PA
CBHW071454080526
44587CB00014B/2100